The People of the River's Mouth

PROJECT SPONSORS

The State Historical Society of Missouri

Special thanks to
Christine Montgomery
Claudia Powell

MISSOURI HERITAGE READERS
General Editor, Rebecca B. Schroeder

Each Missouri Heritage Reader explores a particular aspect of the state's rich cultural heritage. Focusing on people, places, historical events, and the details of daily life, these books illustrate the ways in which people from all parts of the world contributed to the development of the state and the region. The books incorporate documentary and oral history, folklore, and informal literature in a way that makes these resources accessible to all Missourians.

Intended primarily for adult new readers, these books will also be invaluable to readers of all ages interested in the cultural and social history of Missouri.

Other Books in the Series

The People of the River's Mouth

In Search of the
Missouria Indians

Michael Dickey

University of Missouri Press   Columbia and London

Cataloging-in-Publication data available from the Library of Congress
ISBN 978-0-8262-1914-5

∞™ This paper meets the requirements of the
American National Standard for Permanence of Paper
for Printed Library Materials, Z39.48, 1984.

Designer: Kristie Lee
Typesetter: K. Lee Design & Graphics
Printer and binder: Thomson-Shore
Typeface: Palatino

Dedicated to the memory of the Missouria people, the Nyut^achi, who have too long been forgotten to history. I hope this book will help their descendants in the Otoe-Missouria, Ioway, and other American Indian tribes recover a piece of their history. I also dedicate the book to the memory of my grandmother Willa (Plunkett) Simcosky (1899–1982). Her stories about growing up in western Oklahoma instilled in me at an early age a curiosity about and respect for American Indian people, their history, and their cultures.

Contents

Acknowledgments

Many noted anthropologists, historians, and archaeologists, including Francis La Flesche, Alanson Skinner, James Owen Dorsey, George Hyde, Louis B. Houck, Baron Marc Villiers, J. Brewton Berry, Abraham Nasatir, Gilbert Din, John Joseph Mathews, James Mooney, Frederick Webb Hodge, John Swanton, R. David Edmunds, Carl and Eleanor Chapman, Robert Bray, Robert Wiegers, Henry Hamilton, Berlin Basil Chapman, Martha Royce Blaine, Donald Lance, Mildred Mott Widel, Leonard Blake, Michael O'Brien, David J. Costa, Larry Grantham, and Dale Henning have discussed or mentioned the Missouria in their works. The information, while valuable, most often appears in scholarly works or field notes that are not widely accessible. The works themselves often do not include a Native American viewpoint. Primary documents mentioning the Missouria are rare, and they are usually in French or Spanish. This situation has made research for this book especially challenging.

I appreciate the communication that I have had with members of the Otoe-Missouria tribe: Barbara Childs-Walton, Connie Harper, Dawn Briner, Lorena DeRoin, Flo Robedeux, and Bat Shunatona. I gained a vital new perspective on the culture from them. Matthew Jones especially provided assistance with oral traditions, tribal history, and bibliographical materials. Sonny Littlecrow also provided information on oral traditions, tribal history and language concepts. Among members of the Osage tribe, I want to thank Louis F. Burns, who shared his knowledge with me, and Kathryn Red Corn, who gave me access to materials in the Osage tribal museum.

Jimm Goodtracks, Chiwere language preservationist, provided assistance with Ioway-Otoe language and permitted use of ethnographical materials on his website. Dr. Carol Diaz-Granados and James Duncan helped explain Siouan symbolism in the context of modern archaeology; Dr. Lori Stanley, Luther College, and Adam Fracchia provided information in their theses; David Bennett shared newspaper and journal excerpts. Dr. W. Raymond Wood, Professor Emeritus, University of Missouri, Dr. Tim Baumann, Glenn A. Black Laboratory of Archaeology, Dr. R. Bruce McMillan, Director Emeritus, Illinois State Museum, Dr. Jeff Yelton, Central Missouri University, and James Harlan, University of Missouri, provided archaeological and geographical materials and corrections. Tammy Green and Candace Sall, of the University of Missouri, provided access to valuable research materials; Jim Baker, of the Felix Valle, State Historic Site, and Greg Olson, of the Missouri State Archives, and historian Jim Denny also provided needed help. Janet Littlecrow was an encourager and helped open some doors with her husband's tribe.

The research for this publication was made possible by a Brownlee Grant from the State Historical Society of Missouri, Columbia. I am indebted to the society board and to Dr. Gary Kremer for their support. Stephen Chapman permitted use of illustrations done by his mother, Eleanor Chapman. Thanks go to my daughter, Ruth Ellen Bratcher, for maps and graphics work and to the series editor, Rebecca Schroeder, the staff of the University of Missouri Press, and my wife, Diana, for their patience.

The People of the
River's Mouth

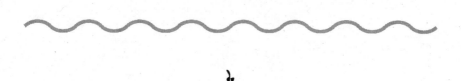

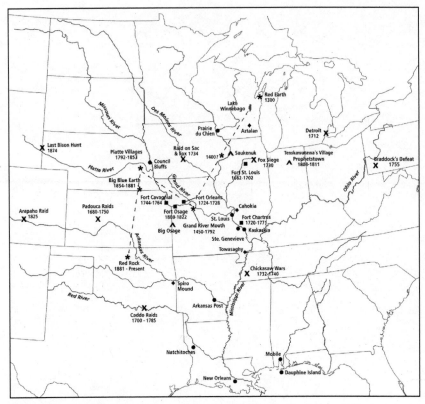

This map shows locations mentioned in relation to the Missouria.
(Courtesy of Ruth Bratcher)

Introduction

The word *Missouri* usually evokes an image of the great western river followed by the Lewis and Clark Expedition or of the midwestern state known for its rolling farmland, forested Ozark hills, and symbolic Gateway Arch. Even Missouri residents seldom associate their state's name with the once-powerful Missouria native nation that gave its name first to the river, then to the state.

Yet for more than a century the tribe played an important role in the commercial and military activities of the "Louisiana Territory," the vast region drained by the Mississippi River and its tributaries, and the "Illinois Country" between Lake Michigan and the Mississippi. Europeans learned of the existence of the Missouria Nation in 1673. The Missouria then numbered in the thousands, but by 1804, fewer than 400 remained, most living with the Otoe Nation. Explorer William Clark described them as "once the most numerous nation in this part of the continent." Scottish naturalist John Bradbury in 1811 called them "once the most powerful nation on the Missouri River." Their numbers continued to dwindle, and a government Indian agent wrote, "Early in 1907, the last full-blooded Missouria Indian died on the Otoe Reservation in Oklahoma, bringing to an end the story of a great and powerful nation." However the agent's statement is not entirely correct. While there are no full-blood Missouria Indians today, some members of the Otoe-Missouria community of Red Rock, Oklahoma, continue to identify their lineage as Missouria. The story of their nation has never been completely told to the general public.

The Missouria had ceased being an independent nation by 1795. Most of their early culture was lost before it could be recorded. They never engaged in a military campaign against the United States. None of their leaders gained the sort of national notoriety accorded those of other tribes, like Tecumseh, Osceola, Sitting Bull, or Geronimo. Consequently, they have been overlooked in history. Their story is like a jigsaw puzzle with many key pieces missing; however, enough information survives to provide some perspective on the Missouria's place in history and an idea of their culture. The discovery of archival materials, improvements in archaeological techniques, and the inclusion of American Indian viewpoints in written history are expanding our knowledge and altering our interpretations. Mistakes are inevitable in this work, and undoubtedly some of my interpretations and theories will prove to be incorrect, but it is not my intention to misrepresent the Missouria or other Indian cultures. Rather, it is my hope that this book will encourage further dialogue and research into the history and culture of the Missouria people.

The Europeans describing the Missouria were not historians, ethnologists, or anthropologists. They were explorers, traders, politicians, and priests interested in the Missouria as trading partners, military allies, or converts to Christianity. Their writings tell us more about their own personal biases than about the Missouria people. The writers often fail to tell us even the names of the Missouria people with whom they dealt. Even those who knew the Missouria well probably did not fully understand their culture. Tribal knowledge was not readily shared with outsiders. Although many aspects of Missouria history are unknown to us, French and Spanish colonial records and the experiences of other Indian nations illustrate the forces of change impacting the Missouria Nation. The late Carl Chapman and the late Robert Bray, both University of Missouri professors, believed that by contrasting the archeological record with the cultures of neighboring and related tribes, it would be possible to reconstruct a likely picture of the Missouria culture.

Historical spellings of tribal names vary greatly and are sometimes unrecognizable. I have provided clarifications in parentheses when needed. To minimize confusion over various references to the state, the river, and the Indian tribe, the historical name "Missouria" will be used for the tribe throughout the text. Further, the alternate but historical names "Illini" refer to the Illinois native nation and "Ioway" to the Iowa native nation. The Winnebago Nation now prefers use of its own name, Ho Chunk.

Quebec, Canada, was established in 1608, and French trappers, traders, and priests spread from there to the Great Lakes and west to the interior of "New France," as they called North America. In 1670,

Father Marquette Descending the Mississippi, 1673. Although he did not meet them, Father Jacques Marquette was the first European to record the existence of the Missouria people. His pronunciation of the Illini word for the Nyut^achi became "Missouri." (Courtesy of the State Historical Society of Missouri)

Father Jacques Marquette, living at a Jesuit mission near present-day Duluth, Minnesota, wrote down accounts of the Mississippi River told to him by visiting Illini Indians. He mentioned a western river that joined the Mississippi and the people living there: "Six or seven days below the Illinois [River] is another river on which are some great nations who use wooden canoes."

Marquette, in company with Louis Jolliet, began a descent of the Mississippi River on June 17, 1673. The men visited an Illini village of eight thousand people in northeast Missouri. This site is now Illiniwek Village State Historic Site, managed by the Missouri Department of Natural Resources. Several days later they arrived at the mouth of a river their Illini guides called *Pekitanoui*. Marquette became the first European to report the existence of the Missouri River:

> As we were gently sailing down the still, clear water, we heard a noise of a rapid into which we were about to fall. I have seen nothing more frightful, a mass of large trees entire with branches, real floating islands came from Pekitanoui, so impetuous that we could not without great danger expose ourselves to pass across. The agitation was so great that the water was all muddy, and could not

> get clear. The Pekitanoui [Missouri] is a considerable river coming from the northwest and empties into the Mississippi. Many towns are located on this river and I hope to make the discovery of the Vermilion or California Sea [Pacific Ocean].

When Marquette asked his guides what people lived on this river, they replied, *"mihsoori"* or *"wemihsoori"* which in their Algonquin language describes a wooden canoe. The Miami tribe for the Missouria used the form *"amihsoolia."* Missouri is therefore interpreted as "people of wood canoes." Marquette wrote the name as "8emess8rit." In seventeenth-century French script the letter "8" was pronounced as a long "o" or "oo" or "w." Ouemessourit was pronounced as Oo-e-mis-oo-ray. Mapmaker Melchisédech Thevenot dropped an "e" and rendered it as "8messourit" (Oumessourit) in 1680. Marquette identified the nearby Osage Nation as "8chage" (Oo-sha-ge). Marquette and Jolliet did not enter the Missouri or meet any of the people dwelling on its banks. French contact with the Missouria was still several years away.

Indian tribes were usually called by the names Europeans put on a map, regardless of whether they were correct. The Missouria were called *Waçuqea* by the Osage and *Wa júqdeã* by the Quapaw, the meanings of which are lost. The Missouria called themselves *Ñutà chi* or *Nyut^achi* (nyu-tah-chee), which has been written as Niut'achi, Ne-o-ge-he, Neojehe, Ne-o-ta-cha and New-dar-cha. Nyut^achi is roughly translated as "People at the River Mouth." Edwin James, botanist and geologist of the Yellowstone Expedition, wrote in 1819 that it meant, "Town at the River's Mouth." Either interpretation is probably a reference to the mouth of the Grand River at the early Missouria villages. Another tradition gives the name as "Those Who Arrive at the Mouth [of a river]." In the Otoe-Missouria-Ioway language *ni* = water; *ut a* = two entities coming together or combining, as in forks of a river; *chi* = to dwell or reside.

Truman Dailey, the last fluent speaker of the Otoe-Missouria language, said that the name Nyut^achi was given to the Missouria after they joined the Otoes. He thought it meant "Those Who Died in the Water," a reference to the near-annihilation of the Missouria when the Sac and Fox tribes ambushed them on the Missouri River. Several tribal groups had a folk explanation for the term as follows: *ni* = water; *u* = in or within; *tà e* = they die; *je`e* = this or these. *Niuta`neje è* would be very similar in pronunciation to *Nyut^achi*, which could account for the conflicting stories of origin.

French Creole traders, *couriers de bois* (woods runners) and *voyageurs* (boatmen), used native place-names or the French pronunciation and translation of those names. Later Anglo-Americans often changed the names altogether. These altered spellings and changes further obscured the meanings of the native names. Indian names often conveyed concepts not readily translated into European languages. As fluency of native languages was lost, so, too, were the meanings of many words and phrases. Today these conditions make it difficult, if not impossible, to translate place-names that are clearly of Missouria origin.

One example of this problem is the Arrow Rock bluff about twenty-five miles southeast of the location of the long-ago Missouria villages. Located on the "Osage Trace," a major Indian trail crossing the Missouri River, this landmark was identified on eighteenth-century French maps as "Pierre à Fleche," literally, "Rock of Arrows." Edwin James explained the origin of the name in 1819: "Arrow Rock is so-called from its having been formerly resorted to by neighboring Indians, for the stone used to point their arrows." The Missouria could have called the bluff *Ma Inno: Ma* = arrow, *Inno* = rock, suggesting a rock or stone shaped like an arrowhead. Another possibility is *Ma Ukan: Ma* = arrow, *Ukan* = a cliff or embankment. However no one can ever be certain of the original Missouria name for the flint-bearing bluff.

On April 9, 1682, René-Robert Cavelier, Sieur de la Salle, who claimed the entire Mississippi River basin for France, named this vast territory Louisiana, in honor of King Louis XIV. In July of 1700, fur trader and explorer Pierre-Charles Le Seur ventured up the "Colbert River" (Mississippi River) to the mouth of the Missouri. He said that the word *Missouri* meant "canoes," so named for the Indians called the "peoples of the canoes." These canoes or dugouts were hewn from gigantic *bax è* (cottonwood), *nathon* (sycamore), or *tage* (walnut) logs, twenty to fifty feet long. They were the only craft that could safely negotiate the hazardous lower Missouri River. Bark canoes like those used on the upper Mississippi River would have been smashed to bits. André Penicault, who kept journals of the early explorations of Louisiana, described how the treacherous nature of the Missouri affected travel: "This river is frightfully swift, especially in the springtime when it is high, for when passing over the islands when it overflows it uproots and carries off the trees. . . . The Indians who live on the banks of the Missouri go up and down it in August when the water is low."

Marquette said that *Pekitanoui* meant, "muddy water" in the Illini language. Father Gabriel Marest confirmed this meaning in 1712. In recent times some have thought Missouri means "Big Muddy," but the correct interpretation of Missouri is certainly "people of wood canoe." Truman Dailey said the Missouri River was called *Nyi soje*, "Smoky Water," perhaps to describe the mist and fog that was frequently suspended above the river or the roiling, cloudy appearance of the suspended silt in the water. Other sources indicate the Missouria, Otoe, and Ioway called the Missouri River *Nyi shujé*, literally, "Red Water." Perhaps this was a reference to the reddish-brown color of the muddy water. The close pronunciation of the two forms and the loss of fluency again demonstrate the difficulty in interpreting Missouria Indian words and phrases.

The word *Missouri* went through many spellings before reaching its current form. Since Marquette's first spelling of Ouemessourit the name of the *Nyut^achi* Nation and their river has appeared in many forms: Emissourita, Wemessouret, Missourita, Massorites, Missourites, Messorites, Misouris, Missoori, Missounta, Missurier, Miss-sou-ly, Mis-sou-li-au, Missurier, Missoury, Missurys, Missuri, Misuris, Mysouri, Musures, Missouries, Missouris, Missourians and Missouria. Eventually "Missouri" came to refer to both the Pekitanoui River and the Nyut^achi Nation, and by the mid-1700s, Pekitanoui had dropped from use.

The Otoe-Missouria adopted Missouria as part of its official tribal name in the 1950s. Truman Dailey and "some other Missouria boys" on the tribal council proposed the name since the Red Rock community was a mix of the two historic tribes. Dailey's father, George Washington Dailey, *Xra Ságe*, Old Eagle, of the Missouria Eagle Clan pronounced it "Mi-zoo-ri-ay." Dailey's father and grandmother taught him about his Missouria heritage, and he, in turn, shared it with Lori Stanley, a doctoral student at the University of Missouri in Columbia. Truman Dailey helped Stanley and the university with a tribal language project in the early 1990s, earning an honorary doctorate degree prior to his death in 1996.

Language is one way of determining relationships among American Indian nations. The Missouria are of the Siouan-language family, speaking a dialect known as Chiwere. Other tribes speaking this dialect were the *Ho Chunk* (Winnebago), the *Wahtohtana* (Otoe), and the *Baxoje* (Ioway). William Clark said these tribes spoke the same language and correctly surmised they were "once one great nation." Edwin James wrote in 1819:

The language of the Otoes, Missouries and Ioways, although the same, is somewhat differently pronounced by these respective nations or tribes. The dialect of the Ioways is more closely allied to that of the Otoes than to the Missouri dialect . . . The Missouri dialect differs in being more nasal; the children however, of this nation being from their residence among the Otoes . . . are gradually assuming the pronunciation of that nation.

The closely related Dhegiha Siouan-dialect group includes the Osage, Kansa (Kaw), Omaha, Ponca, and Quapaw. The divergence between Dhegiha and Chiwere dialects is greater, although they have some words in common. William Clark observed some similarities in 1804. Linguists believe the two dialects began diverging sometime between A.D. 400 and 1000. Because of some broad similarities in language and culture, the Chiwere- and Dhegiha-speaking tribes are sometimes collectively referred to as Southern Siouans.

A comparison of some common words from Siouan tribes helps demonstrate this linguistic relationship.

	Horse	House	Foot	Sun	Bone	Two	Three
Otoe-Missouria	sunge	chi	thi	bi	wahu	nuwe	daani
Ioway	shunye	chi	thi	bi	wahu	nuwe	daani
Ho Chunk	shuuk	cii	sii	wii	wahuu	nuupe	taani
Osage	shonka	tsi	si	mi	wahu	dhompa	dhaabri
Dakota Sioux	shunka	tipi	si	wi	huhu	numpa	yamni

Northern Siouans include the Dakota (Santee), Nakota (Yankton) and Lakota (Teton) Sioux, Hidatsa (Minetaree), Assiniboin, Mandan, and Crow (Absaroka). Siouan speakers scattered across the southeastern United States included the Biloxi, Saponi, Tutelo, Monacan, Manahoac, and Catawba.

Communication between the Missouria and their non-Siouan-speaking neighbors was not difficult. Sign language, *nàwe arè i kichèwi ke* (speak to each other using hands), was a universal form of communication. Many tribes also spoke the languages of their allies and trading partners. Adoptions and intermarriage with other tribes helped bridge the language differences. In the eighteenth century, many Missouria learned to speak French, and they continued using French rather than English long after the Americans arrived in the nineteenth century.

1

The Origins of the Missouria
Woodland, Mississippian, and Oneota Cultures

Oral tradition among the Missouria included creation stories that accounted for the tribe's origin. Combined with oral history, archaeology provides a method for tracing the historical roots of an ethnic group. Archeologically the Missouria are considered direct descendants of the Oneota. It was originally thought that the Oneota were the final phase of, or an outgrowth of, the Mississippian culture, which flourished from about A.D. 900 to 1500. The general consensus today is that the Oneota, especially the Missouria and other Chiwere-speaking tribes, developed from Woodland cultures in the upper Midwest around A.D. 1000. While contemporaneous with the Mississippian culture and perhaps influenced by it, the Oneota had an independent history but eventually succeeded and perhaps absorbed some of the Mississippians in much of the region.

The Mississippian civilization thrived along the great river systems of the central United States. Mississippians were a sedentary people, meaning their settlements were permanent. Mississippian towns featured large plazas and extensive, complex ceremonial and burial mounds made of earth and encircled by residential areas. Some of the highest mounds show evidence of having been homes of prominent leaders and their families, who were treated as descendants of a deity. Mississippians relied mainly on farming rather than hunting and gathering food. Archaeological evidence shows that maize (corn) was the staple crop and a variety of beans, squash, and pumpkins were also grown. The notched flint hoe was the primary agricultural tool. Hunters living in smaller outlying villages harvested game such as deer and bear and shipped the processed meat and hides to the larger towns.

Trade materials from across the North American continent reached their towns, including seashells from the Pacific and Gulf coasts, copper from the Great Lakes, obsidian flint from Idaho, and turquoise and pottery from the desert Southwest. In addition, some art forms, spiritual concepts, and ideas appear to have been shared via these trade networks.

The women made a wide variety of shell-tempered pottery that included jars, pots, plates, and bowls, some of it elaborately decorated. Ground mussel shells were added to the clay, which was then baked, to give a vessel more durability. Some of these ceramics have the shape of animals such as frogs, bears, dogs, bats, birds, snakes, or human heads and supernatural creatures. Many of these were made

These two small Oneota vases were found near Malta Bend in 1932. The vase on the right shows ground-up mussel shells that add strength to the clay before baking. The Missouria continued making pots and vases similar to these even after trade with Europeans began. (Carl H. Chapman, *The Archaeology of Missouri, II*, courtesy of the State Historical Society of Missouri)

for specific sacred purposes. Even ceramics and earthenware made for everyday use were probably purposeful and reflective of the oral traditions of the people. Specialization in agriculture allowed skilled craftsmen, artisans, and tradesmen to develop in Mississippian society. Large numbers of flint blades and points, too finely finished and delicate to be used for hunting or warfare, were made for ceremonial use. Sheets of copper were made into ceremonial ornaments or detailed bas-relief plaques illustrating figures of legend and ceremonial importance. Some of these Mississippian art and ceremonial forms carried over into Oneota culture.

The Mississippians were a culture, not a tribe. They were probably not a unified people and likely spoke diverse languages. Their towns may have been like city-states, sometimes cooperating, sometimes competing with one another. Mississippians had sophisticated and complex religious and social structures based on the movements of constellations and the changing seasons. Figures on their pottery and copper bas-relief provide a good idea of their appearance and personal ornamentation, but despite abundant archaeological material, many aspects of their civilization remain a matter of speculation.

One of the great economic, political, and religious centers of Mississippian culture was the mound city at what is now Cahokia, Illinois. At its peak Cahokia contained over 200 mounds and 30,000 to 40,000 inhabitants, making it the largest Indian settlement north of Mexico. Cahokia State Historic Site, managed by the Illinois Historical Agency, has been declared a World Heritage Site. St. Louis, Missouri, was once nicknamed the "Mound City" because of the large number of Mississippian mounds there; however, all but one of these mounds have been destroyed by development. In 2009 the Osage Nation of Oklahoma purchased the last of them, Sugar Loaf Mound, to preserve it. Another major Mississippian town near New Madrid, Missouri, is preserved as Towasaghy State Historic Site and managed by the Missouri Department of Natural Resources. Towasaghy means "Old Town" in the Osage language, although there is no tribal memory of its being occupied. The northernmost Mississippian complex is preserved in the 172-acre Aztalan State Park in southeastern Wisconsin. This complex may have influenced the development of the Oneota people who eventually became the Missouria, Ho Chunk, Otoe, and Ioway nations.

Mississippian towns show evidence of wood stockades with guard towers. The settlements may have been threatened by Indians from other towns or by nomadic bands. The towns were declining before the arrival of Europeans, and Cahokia appears to have been abandoned well before A.D. 1500. Environmental conditions may have contributed to the problem of growing enough food to sustain the large population centers. However it seems evident that the arrival of Europeans on the continent and the new diseases they brought hastened the final breakup and demise of the Mississippian towns.

Coinciding with the decline of the Mississippian towns was the rise of Oneota villages. Again the term *Oneota* describes a cultural group, not a tribe. Residents of small, scattered villages could more easily secure food from hunting and gathering, especially in the event of crop failure. The Oneota spread west from the Great Lakes area onto the prairies and plains to hunt bison. They continued farming, but hoes made of bison scapula replaced notched flint as the primary farming tool. Oneota women made shell-tempered pottery, but the

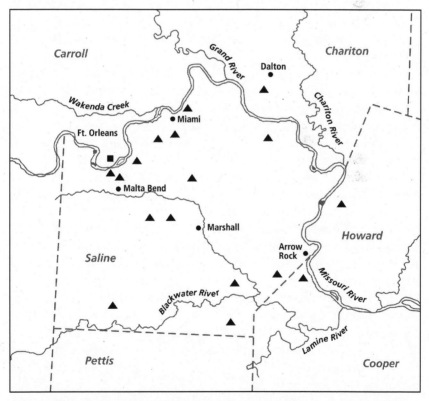

This map shows the approximate locations of key Oneota and Missouria archaeological sites in the vicinity of Saline County, Missouri. (Courtesy of Ruth Bratcher)

forms were more utilitarian and somewhat less ornate than Mississippian ceramics. The Oneota were a semisedentary people. Their villages were occupied seasonally instead of year-round, primarily during the spring planting and the autumn harvest. The remainder of the year the Oneota spread out in clan groups, hunting or gathering edible plants. Deep cache pits were dug in the villages for storing dried corn for winter use. If the contents spoiled, the pits were then used for trash. These trash pits provide valuable information about the diet and lifestyle of the Oneota.

Villages were periodically relocated to access new resources. The Oneota cultural area was roughly bounded by the Missouri River valley in the west, the Minnesota River in the north, Lake Michigan in the east, and the St. Louis-Cahokia area in the south. The Oneota remained connected to a continental trade network, but it had also declined. Oneota sites contain some exotic materials but not in the abundance found at Mississippian sites. Such a decline would be normal in a transition from a centralized sedentary farming society to a decentralized semisedentary hunting and gathering society.

Many of the known Oneota sites in the state of Missouri are located on the south side of the Missouri River. Around A.D. 1450 a large Oneota village was established in present-day northern Saline County, Missouri, near Miami. This location comprises a series of high loess bluffs on the Missouri River, locally known as the "Pinnacles." Loess is an accumulation of windblown soil deposited as glaciers retreated during the last ice age, about 15,000 years ago.

This Oneota site is known as the Utz site, for the family that once owned and farmed the area. The Utz site is considered the premier Oneota site within Missouri. There are other and earlier Oneota sites in Saline County but none as large or as continuously occupied. The known boundary of the site encompasses over 300 acres, and it has been declared a National Historic Landmark. About half of it is protected within Van Meter State Park and administered by the Missouri Department of Natural Resources. The site coincides well with the location of the "Oumessourit" village identified on the maps of Father Marquette in 1673, Jean Baptiste Franquelin in 1684, and Guillaume DeLisle in 1718. The presence of European artifacts confirms some intermittent occupation of the site continued during the early trade period, possibly as late as 1723.

The location of Utz and other Oneota sites in the Midwest also coincides well with the migration traditions of the Otoe, Missouria, and Ioway. This tradition indicates an origin of the Chiwere-speaking people on the south shore of Green Bay in present-day Wisconsin. This area was called *Máyaⁿ shúje* (Red Earth). The clans came together and dwelt there before eventually becoming the tribes we know today. Major Jonathan Bean recorded a story told to him by an old, unnamed Otoe chief in 1826, here edited for ease of reading:

> Long before the white man came to the country a large band of Indians, who inhabited the northern Great Lakes, being discontented, concluded that they would migrate to the southwest in pursuit of the buffalo. Near Lake Winnebago [Wisconsin] they divided, and the Ho Chunk [Winnebago] remained at Green Bay. The rest proceeded to the Mississippi River then followed it south. One band concluded to remain near the mouth of the Rock River. These were the Baxoje [Ioway] the Grey Snow People. The rest of the group continued southwest and reached the Missouri River at the mouth of the Grand River where they formed a large village. The peace of the village was disrupted by a quarrel. A young man of prominent family sought the marriage of a woman of similar family, but her family rejected the bridal payments. In defiance the young couple ran off together in the nearby forest. This was a serious breech of the formal marriage relationship. Learning of the relationship, the girl's father became angry. and threatened to attack the young man's family. However, the families and their followers, who separated into two distinct groups, settled the matter. One part of the village followed the young man and his kinsmen up the Missouri River. The young woman left her family and joined her lover. Because of this those who journeyed upstream were known as Wahtohtana "Those Who Make Love" (Otoes). They eventually settled near the Nemaha River and later, the Platte River. Those who stayed behind received the name Ñútá chi or Nyut^achi "People Dwelling [Where] Rivers Fork."

An Ioway tradition said the separation of the Missouria and Otoe happened at the confluence of the Missouri and Mississippi rivers. Each clan had its own version of events. The variances in these traditions were of no consequence to the Missouria, Otoe, and Ioway. It was how they remembered events, they would simply say. Hundreds of years had passed between the time the migrations began and the time the stories were collected. Extended memories had faded and become clouded. In comparison, even modern archaeologists have differing theories of Oneota origins and migrations.

There are twenty-eight known Oneota sites in Saline County alone, although they may not all be connected to the Missouria. As the

Chiwere speakers moved down from the north, the Dhegiha speakers probably moved up the Missouri River. No one is certain how rapidly these migrations occurred. The Chiwere- and Dhegiha-speaking groups undoubtedly interacted and moved multiple times prior to being "discovered" by Europeans as the tribes we know today. Besides the Utz site, Gumbo Point, eight miles to the west, was occupied starting around 1714. The smaller Utlaut archaeological site nearby may represent a clan or transitional village site. Gumbo Point and Utlaut are in the high bottomland prairie that is known today as the Pettisaw or Petit Osage Plains. The Petit (Little) Osage tribe also had a large village here that today is known as the Plattner archaeological site.

Archaeologists, beginning in 1906 with Gerard Fowke, have conducted extensive studies of the Utz site. The Utlaut and Gumbo Point sites have been less studied. About 90 percent of the Gumbo Point site was destroyed by river channelization and levee projects in the 1930s. J. M. "Buster" Crick, a founding member of the Missouri Archaeological Society, salvaged Gumbo Point artifacts during the channelization project, which are now on display at Arrow Rock State Historic Site. Other Oneota sites in Saline and Howard counties contain European trade materials but the sites have not been investigated enough to make any interpretation about their possible connection to any other historic tribe. However, it seems likely that some of these, as well as perhaps still undiscovered sites, are connected to the Missouria. A site in Chariton County examined by the National Park Service in 2009 may have connection to an "ancient village" of the Missouria mentioned by William Clark in 1804.

Some archaeologists think that the Missouria arrived at an already occupied Utz site. If this is the case, the Utz or the nearby earlier Guthrey site may be connected to the Dhegiha Siouan people, perhaps the early Osage. In 1699, Father Jean St. Cosmé wrote that the Osage had moved from the Missouri to the river that bore their name. Whether this was a seasonal or a permanent migration is not clear. The Little Osage especially show connection to the Orr Phase of Oneota culture and resided on the Missouri River until the late eighteenth century. Regardless of its origin, the Utz site clearly is connected to the early Missouria and demonstrates how they lived. Cultural patterns at Oneota sites throughout the Midwest are remarkably consistent, and the Missouria were definitely the last people to occupy the Utz site.

A prominent feature at the Utz site is an earthwork commonly known as the "Old Fort." Located on a ridge next to the village site,

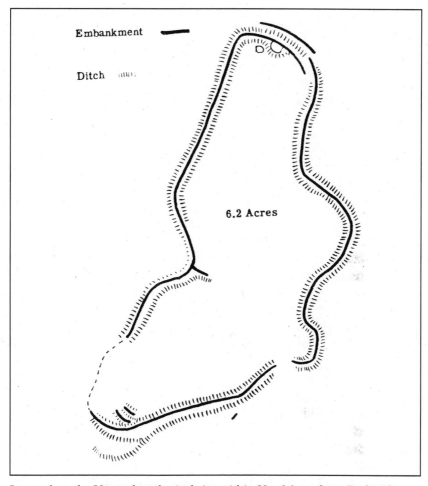

Located on the Utz archaeological site within Van Meter State Park, "the Old Fort," as shown in this diagram consisted of a continuous ditch and embankments enclosing six acres. Indians of the Woodland cultural period were well known as mound builders and at first were believed to have constructed it. However excavations in 1970 showed that the Missouria Indians had constructed the feature on top of an earlier Woodland site. It's exact purpose remains a matter of speculation. (Courtesy of the State Historical Society of Missouri)

it is 1,000 feet long by 420 feet wide. W. Raymond Wood cut a trench through the north end of the feature in 1970 and determined the Oneota Missouria constructed it on top of a Woodland period site. The area is heavily timbered now, but soil profiles show the area was originally prairie. Originally, the perimeter ditches were six feet deep and the embankments were four feet high, suggesting that the earth-work could have been a defensive position to retreat to in the event of an attack. Indian fortifications usually had log palisades, but no evidence of postholes was found in the trench. It could have been a ceremonial area or possibly a lacrosse field. *Táwe,* lacrosse games, were played across North America and were far more than mere rec-reation. Ceremony and ritual preparation by the players preceded the games.

The Utz site demonstrates the transition from a Neolithic (Stone Age) culture to one that had acquired metal tools and implements through trade. Flint and bone weapons and tools decline when those made of iron, copper, and brass increase. This transition is not always distinct where the site has been excavated, but the relatively thin layer of trade materials indicates the Utz site was abandoned fairly soon after trade with Europeans began.

There are no creation stories that survive directly from early Mis-souria tradition. However, those of the related Otoe, Ioway, and Ho Chunk are similar enough to give a plausible idea of Missouria con-cepts. Mythology is a body of folklore, legends, and beliefs, often with ties to documented history, that a culture uses to explain its origins, natural events, and human behavior. In contemporary American so-ciety, myth is sometimes interpreted to mean a story with no basis in fact. However, use of the term here merely refers to the original definition. The "mythical time" in Siouan cultures simply refers to the time before humans, when they believed only supernatural be-ings and monstrous creatures inhabited the earth.

It is important to note that there are usually variations by clan of the same stories. Again the variations and disparities were of no consequence to the Missouria, Otoe, and Ioway. Truman Dailey once told an Otoe-Missouria creation story. It probably contains more Otoe than Missouria influence but still provides insight as to how the Mis-souria viewed their origins. Here it is edited for clarity:

> Nothing existed in the beginning, except an abundance of water. It flowed everywhere pushing all life out of it. In time land ap-peared. Vegetation sprouted and forests grew to towering heights. Animals and birds dwelt in these forests and all life spoke the same language. From the life-giving waters the Bear Clan rose and came ashore, thinking they were the first people. But they were dismayed when they saw other tracks on the shore leading away from the water. The Bear Clan chased the Beaver Clan, whom they caught and intended to kill. The Beaver Clan was a diplomatic people and

suggested to the Bear that they become brothers because life alone was so hard. The Bears agreed and the two clans lived in harmony, thinking they were the only people on the earth. Then they discovered the Elk. The Elks proposed that they become brothers, and the Bear and Beaver accepted them. The Sky People came through the sky opening and swooped down to earth where they found signs of the other three clans. The Eagles approached them as friends and again the number of clans grew. Each clan had knowledge that could be shared to help all of the clans. They called upon Wakanda the Creator to teach them how to live. He gave them a sacred pipe and gave each clan special knowledge and rights for using the pipe. The Buffalo, Snake, Owl and Pigeon Clans had their own sacred pipe. They offered their pipe in friendship to the others but the Bear rejected it. Eventually the Bear's heart softened and the two groups accepted each other's pipes, a sign of friendship and peaceful co-existence. This was how everything began.

Anthropology student William Whitman stayed with the Otoe-Missouria in Oklahoma in 1935. He recorded a fragment of a sub-clan creation story that he attributed to the "Missouri Bear." This possibly represents a tradition surviving from Missouria Bear Clan members who had merged with the Otoe Bear Clan:

> The Bear lived in the water, which was covered with ice. When the ice melted the Bear came out on dry land and ate the fruit that Wakanda had created. The four Bear brothers heard thunder and a great storm of wind and rain came. The thunder was the Eagle Clan. The Bears and Eagles met one another and became friends. The Bear gave the Eagle a pipe and the Eagle gave the Bear a wing. They made a pact and agreed to have their children intermarry. They went buffalo hunting and Bear took the lead. The Bear showed the people how to butcher the buffalo and prepare the meat and hide.

Events from the mythical time such as this were handed down by oral tradition, and they shaped the social and religious structures of the tribe. The origin stories remain timeless and always relevant in promoting the identity and cohesion of the clans. The stories of the mythical time were not necessarily viewed as literal events. They were often allegorical in nature, describing the human condition and providing instruction in moral conduct and social behavior.

The clan formed the fundamental building block of tribal organization. The Missouria, Otoe, and Ioway were each a confederation of family clans. Each clan was based on a spirit animal that had made a significant contribution to the people in the days of creation. The clan connected the people to the natural world and gave them insight into the supernatural world. The gathering of all the clans for ceremonial purposes represented the completeness and balance of the universe as they understood it. The clan included an extended family of relatives who shared the division of labor, looked after the well-being of all its members, and educated the young in community values and spirituality. Within clans people did not intermarry, thus preventing inbreeding.

Each clan had its elders, who functioned as advisors. These were usually men, but sometimes women became elders. They possessed sacred knowledge of the ceremonies, traditions, and history of the clan. This information was only shared with members of the same clan. Even if other clan members (such as elders' spouses) knew this information, they had no right to speak of it. The elders sought visions or received guidance from their spirit guardians. They met in council with other clan leaders during their season to lead and through their accumulated wisdom deliberated on the course of events for the clan and tribe. They formed the underlying basis for tribal government, a system that was often unknown to Europeans and, later, to American officials.

The preferable term for a leader in traditional Otoe-Missouria society is *wá eghi* (headman). The English word *chief* was a term assigned by Europeans, who incorrectly assumed these leaders had powers similar to those of monarchs. The position of headman in the early times was said to be hereditary. Becoming a headman was not easy for a member of the leading family. A headman was expected to be a valorous warrior, kind, generous, impartial in resolving disputes, and leading by personal example rather than by authoritarian dictate —in short, to fill the role of a father to his people.

There were various categories of headmen in Otoe, Missouria, and Ioway society. There were leaders in governance, medicine, war, and spiritual matters. Europeans described leaders with titles like "head chief," "principal chief" "grand chief" "inferior chief" "lead chief" "first chief" "second chief" "band chief" "war chief" or "village chief." It is difficult to correlate these terms with the actual leadership structure of Southern Siouans. Europeans also interfered with the leadership structure by giving special gifts and medals to individuals who were not hereditary leaders. Their aim was to buy favors and gain influence over the tribe by recognizing "chiefs." This often led to political friction and caused splits within tribes. The Spanish in 1773 reported that a Missouria hunter sought to usurp his "village chief's" authority, a serious breach of protocol and tribal custom. He did this by accepting presents from traders and dividing them among his followers; he then claimed that he was of "noble birth" and thus had the right to be a headman.

Especially skilled hunters might be appointed to act as *wán wikida*, "camp protectors" or leaders, for a buffalo hunt. Their authority was unquestioned for the duration of the hunt. The *waakida*, or soldiers, enforced the hunt orders and whipped disobedient persons whose behavior jeopardized a hunt. While it seems harsh, an overeager hunter could endanger the welfare of the entire tribe. A warrior might receive a vision directing him to go to war or to avenge the death of a relative. With the sanction of the elders he could raise a war party. However, these war leaders, soldiers, and camp protectors lost their authority and resumed their ordinary status within the tribe once their mission was completed.

In Southern Siouan societies, there were two grand divisions, which anthropologists labeled "moieties." The Sky clans formed the Upper, or Sky, moiety, and the others formed the Lower, or Earth, moiety. The Earth moiety is also associated with water. The Southern Siouans saw duality and balance in the universe, as natural events and behaviors occurred in pairs. For example, night and day, winter and summer, earth and sky, life and death, storms and calm, happiness and sadness, good and evil, success and failure, and war and peace all balanced one another. This balance was carried out in the leadership structure by the division into the Sky and Earth people. Villages were divided by an east-to-west lane representing the path of the sun, the giver of life. The Sky people lived in the northern half of the village and the Earth people in the southern half.

Richard Shunatona, an Otoe-Missouria elder, told William Whitman that from the month of *Makake* (they dig the earth), April, to *Takiruxe* (deer mate), October, the Otoe tribe was led by the Buffalo Clan. The remainder of the year the Bear Clan led. The bear came from below this earth, and the buffalo came down from the sky, and the shared power of the Buffalo and Bear clans assured harmony and balance within the tribe. The Osage system had two leaders from each division who led simultaneously, the Sky "chief" presiding in civil matters and the Earth "chief" in military matters. In turn, they would convene councils with the clan elders. The Missouria followed a dual leadership pattern, and the system may have adapted as changes in their population occurred. Whether the early Missouria copied the dual Osage model of civil and military leaders or held to the Otoe-Ioway model of seasonal leadership is unknown.

Little is known directly about the Missouria clan system before they joined the Otoes. Afterward they continued to function independently within Otoe society, but as the Missouria intermarried with the Otoe clan differences gradually changed. Under each clan were at least four subclans, but these were no longer recognized by 1900. For example, under the Otoe Bear clan there were four subclans: Sacred Black Bear, Bear with Spotted Breast, White Nose Bear, and Little Bear. James Owen Dorsey recorded the clans of the Chiwere tribes in 1879. Dorsey's field notes in the National Anthropological Archives describe how clans were divided between moieties. Gaps in the Missouria clan system are undoubtedly similar to those known to exist in related tribes.

Clans in parentheses in the following table were already gone by 1879.

Missouria	Otoe	Ioway	Ho Chunk
	Upper Moiety or Sky People		
Thunderbird	Thunderbird	Thunderbird	Thunderbird
	(The Thunderbird was a spiritual being with no earthly counterpart, but similar to an eagle)		
Eagle	Eagle	Eagle	Eagle
	(They made *Itado*, friendship, with the Bear clan so also became part of the earth people)		
Hawk?	Owl	Owl	Hawk
Small Bird?	Pigeon	Pigeon	Pigeon
Buffalo	Buffalo	Buffalo	Buffalo
	Lower Moiety or Earth People		
Elk	Elk	Elk	Elk-Deer
Black Bear	Black Bear	Black Bear	Bear
(Wolf)	Wolf	Wolf	Wolf
(Beaver)	Beaver	Beaver	Water Spirit
(Snake)	(Snake)	(Snake)	Snake-Fish

Naming ceremonies were times of celebration and ceremony in the clan. Besides birth-order names, individuals might receive different names throughout their lives, names reflecting notable incidents in their lives. Each one superseded a previous name, although none in good standing were discarded. Hereditary names were also passed down. Truman Dailey was named *Mashi Manyi*, Soaring High, an Eagle Clan name. He was also called *Sunge Hka*, White Horse, the name of his grandfather, who was a distinguished headman. Europeans and Americans misinterpreted honorary titles such as that of "Big Soldier," *Maya*ⁿ*kida Xashe* (Great Guardian of the Land), believing they were personal names. They tried to spell phonetically names they could not pronounce, from a language that is not written and they often completely missed the meaning when translating. The multiplicity of names and honorary titles combined with mistranslations can make it difficult to identify with certainty individuals mentioned in explorers' journals and government records.

William Whitman also recorded fragments of the "Missouri Bear" clan naming ceremony. Again this may be from the remnants of Missouria tradition incorporated into the Otoe. Names were a word picture for framing the child's character and his parents' and clan's hopes for his future. A man who knew the rituals and was properly authorized selected the name of a child. This was accomplished by learning of the child's manner, by meditation, and by prayer. If the father knew the rituals and had the right to do so, he could select the name himself. A lodge was set up, and only clan members were permitted to attend the ceremony. Ceremonial prayer songs were sung. When the child was brought in, the clan members sang a sacred song, each of them holding sacred tobacco in one hand, and asked Wakanda and the Sacred Grandfather Spirits Above for blessings. Then they placed the tobacco in the fire as an offering. The name-giver had a pile of sticks that represented different names, and the majority of clan members had to reach agreement on the name given to the child. Each name had its own special song.

Children were important to the Missouria, as to all Indian nations. They have always represented the tribes' future and served as the receptacles in which ancient knowledge and traditions are passed down. The Southern Siouan cultures were patrilineal societies, meaning the lineage of a child was determined through the father's clan. They were matrilocal in nature, meaning the father lived with his wife's family. Maternal grandparents, aunts, and uncles played important roles in rearing and instructing the children.

Uncles (the mother's brothers) instructed their nephews in hunting and often accompanied them on their first war journeys. Boys were encouraged to wrestle, hold footraces, and play games like *howé kuje,* or "hoop and spear." In this game each boy tried to hurl a spear or shoot an arrow through a rolling hoop. It is thought that several round stones excavated on the Utz site served a similar purpose. The sides of the stones were concave, and the boys would have tried to hit the sides of a stone as it rolled along the ground. They would also hunt small game like birds and rabbits. Girls played with dolls and learned from their aunts and older sisters how to sew, dress hides, and tend gardens. These activities presented social outlets for the girls and taught them skills that would contribute to the welfare of their families, clan, and ultimately their tribe. Boys and girls played together until they were about eleven years old; then they were separated. Children always had a complete support network of both their maternal and paternal relatives. Corporal punishment was unknown.

Jean Baptiste Truteau, a trader on the Missouri River, wrote in 1795 about childbirth among the Missouri River tribes. "When a woman [was] about to give birth she withdrew to a small hut built for that purpose, attended by some of the older women of the village." The mother "was seldom laid up with child birth more than two days," whereupon she returned to the encampment and resumed her daily tasks. The day after the child was born it was washed and strapped to a cradleboard.

The Missouria were polygamous, and a man might have more than one wife. Women were allowed to have only one husband at a time. A brother-in-law or another male relative would care for a woman who lost her husband. Often the brother-in-law would take her as a wife. A common misperception by Europeans was that the Indian women were merely domestic slaves and the men were lazy. However, both sexes played equally vital roles in ensuring the survival of the family, the clan, and the tribe. Women owned the lodges and all the property they contained. A woman could divorce her husband for just cause simply by throwing his belongings out the lodge door.

Their system produced a strong social order, providing stability and continuity within the tribe. The family circle remained intact even when one of its members died. Ceremonies reinforced the family and clan structure and further helped bind the family by creating a strong sense of identity and a spiritual bond with their ancestors and with future generations.

Spirituality pervaded all aspects of Missouria life. One example is a mother painting a red stripe down the part of her daughter's hair. The stripe represents the path of the sun, the giver of life. The east, or sunrise, represents the dawning of day, the beginning of life; the west, or sunset, represents twilight, the end of life. All of life traveled this path, and the Missouria kept this in mind. Villages also divided on this east-west path of the sun. The north half of the village was composed of Sky clans; the south half was composed of Earth clans. (Drawing by Eleanor Chapman, from Carl H. and Eleanor F. Chapman, *Indians and Archaeology of Missouri*, revised edition, courtesy of the State Historical Society of Missouri and Stephen Chapman.)

A profound spirituality permeated all aspects of Southern Siouan cultures. Otoe, Ioway, Ho Chunk, Osage, Kansa, Ponca, Quapaw, and Omaha traditions demonstrate some common spiritual themes also present in traditions of the Missouria. Contrasting the fragmentary European reports with surviving Indian traditions and archaeological records provides some basis for interpretation of Missouria beliefs. There were three levels of the universe: the Above World (sky), the Middle World (where humans dwell), and the Lower World (below the earth). The Above and Lower worlds were subdivided into different tiers or levels. The Otoe, Missouria, and Ioway believed in one omnipotent being from which all creation flowed. Originally this power was termed *Máun*, Earth Maker or Creator, a term still used by the Ho Chunk today. Perhaps influenced by early Jesuit missionaries, the Otoe, Missouria, and Ioway began to use one manifestation in lieu of *Máun*. This was *Wakanda,* the Supreme Being whose presence was everywhere, in both animate and inanimate objects. Wakanda was not directly approachable, but he communicated to human beings through visions and through the visible forces of nature.

The Missouria, Otoe, and Ioway recognized a number of Holy Spirit Beings, similar to angels in Christianity. These beings helped create or maintain order in the universe; for instance, *Tuhi Dowe,* the Four Wind Grandfathers, represented the cardinal directions of north, south, east, and west. Some spirit beings were messengers from Wakanda; others could be used by Wakanda as agents of good or evil. Still others were tricksters doing either good or harm, depending on the situation in which they were encountered. *Ischexi,* the horned water panthers, were Lower World beings that dwelt in water and bore characteristics of both panthers (mountain lions) and serpents; they often had buffalo horns or deer antlers. These water spirits inhabited the whirlpools of large rivers, which were doorways to the Lower World. Sometimes they could be seen sunning themselves on the riverbanks. Southern Siouans took great pains not to offend these or any other sacred beings.

Dreams and visions gave some tribal members insight into the spirit world. Secluding oneself and fasting under the guidance of a mentor was the common way to seek a vision. A spirit in the form of a clan animal often appeared, bringing the sought-after message. Sometimes spiritual assistance came when it was not sought, and stories of such occurrences continue among the Otoe-Missouria and Ioway today. An example is this Otoe tradition handed down from the nineteenth century:

On one long ago occasion an ill woman wondered away from a hunting camp. She rested by a creek for some time until she recovered. In the meantime the camp had moved to a new location. The group assumed she had gone off to die. When she returned to the campsite she found it abandoned and [saw] that someone else had died and was buried there. Because she was hungry, she ate a bowl of meat left for the dead person and began to follow the trail. On the prairie she lost the trail and became disoriented in a heavy fog. She heard someone and went to the sound. The prairie grass was high, but as she came upon a gray figure sitting in the grass, smoke was coming from its mouth. When she realized it was a grizzly bear, she became frightened, believing she was about to die. The bear was smoking a pipe and called out to her, "Daughter don't be afraid for I have come to help you get back to your people." The bear told her to follow him, and when he walked she walked, and when he trotted she trotted. Her strength returned and finally the bear stopped and said "I have brought you this far, now you will get home." The bear warned her she would meet two people on the trail, but she was to go around them and not speak to them because they were dead. Soon she came to a person on the trail but talked to him. She recognized him, and he said, "I have died and now I'm trying to come back to life." Farther up the trail she met another man and talked to him as well. He too had died and was trying to come back to life. Suddenly her strength left her and she became very weak because she had talked with the dead men. However, she reached the village and soon recovered. In later years, she took up smoking to honor the grizzly bear spirit that had saved her. She also began to doctor and heal others with bear medicine.

Sacred pipes have been an important part of American Indian cultures for well over three thousand years. Archaeologists have found an extensive variety of pipe bowls on the Utz site. Sacred pipes held spiritual significance hearkening back to the mythical time when the clans appeared. Only older people used small pipes for recreational smoking along with prayers, as did the woman saved by the bear. Young men did not inhale smoke except as part of a prayer ceremonial. Some pipe bowls recovered from the Utz site are made of limestone. Most of them are made of Catlinite, a red claylike substance that hardens and can be polished like marble. Catlinite was traded across the continent, but it is found only in one location—in southwestern Minnesota. The quarry there has long been regarded as sacred ground by Native Americans and is protected by the National

Park Service as Pipestone National Monument. Only American Indians with a certified permit can quarry the stone there.

Smoking the pipe, or the "calumet," as the French called it, marked all solemn occasions and ceremonies. Native-grown tobacco, sweet grass, cedar, and sage are sacred plants. Tobacco is still burned as an offering to Wakanda and Holy Grandfather Spirits. Father Marest wrote from the Illinois Country in 1700 that there two kinds of calumets. One was for peace and one was for war, and they were distinguished by the colors of feathers that adorned them. The Father's description of the pipes may have applied more to the Illini than to the Missouria or Osage, though they were probably similar. In 1721, fur trader Pierre Deliette reported that the Missouria, Little Osage, and the Illini "sang the calumet" together every year to honor their friendship and renew their alliance. A headman would hold the pipe aloft in his hands and sing; others would answer in chorus while dancing to a drum. Trader Pierre de Charlevoix briefly described this complex "Pipe Dance," which the Missouria called *wááyanwe*, "sing over them":

> They [Missouria and Osage] never fail every year to come among them [Illini] and to bring them the calumet, which is the symbol of peace among all the nations. . . . Good cheer is not lacking on their arrival, and later in the same evening they go off to the cabin of the one to whom they are to give the calumet and sing until day. They do this four nights consecutively, after which they make scaffolds outside if it is fine weather and go in search of the man or of his wives to whom they sing the calumet, and they take him up on this scaffold and all place themselves beside him and beat drums and shake their rattles and sing all day long. Two of them push him gently to and fro between them as a still more significant mark of the honor they do him. During all this time everybody comes to strike a post, which has been planted purposely, to recite his exploits, and afterwards they give gifts in such degree as each one can and in accordance with the honor deserved by the one to whom they sing . . . this calumet is made . . . of a red stone that is found in the direction of the Sioux. It has a very long handle, from which are hung several feathers painted red, yellow, and black, brought together in the form of a fan. This handle is moreover covered with the skins of ducks' necks. During the whole time consumed by the singing, one of them holds the calumet, which he shakes continually before the one to whom it is given. They cease to sing when they see that no one comes any longer to strike the post. They then escort their chief to his cabin and leave him the calumet and sev-

eral beaver skins or skins of bears, bucks, or cats. The ones who accompany him sometimes receive a load of merchandise. When they return this compliment it gives pleasure to the Illini.

Along with the sacred pipes each clan had *warúxawe*. These sacred bundles were wrapped in leather and contained consecrated articles for tribal prayer ceremonies. The articles might have appeared as commonplace stones, feathers, claws, bits of hair, or even the mummified skin of a bird, but clan elders knew the specific spiritual meaning of each item, as with Christians knowing the story of the crucifix gives the object spiritual significance. Sacred bundles contained spiritual power so were cared for responsibly by their keepers and were not opened without need. Different bundles had different functions, such as healing arts, defense in warfare, or success in hunting.

The Missouria connection to Mississippian and Oneota traditions can be deduced from sacred symbolism. An example is found with ivorybill and pileated woodpeckers. In the Osage and Omaha belief system the birds inspired courage through their strength and endurance, as exemplified by their hammering wood all day without ill effect. They were wary birds, difficult to approach and speedy in flight. They bore the colors of war: red represented the color of all-consuming fire; black represented the destruction caused by fire; and white represented the purity of spirit a warrior had to possess to stay in harmony with the cosmos since death would disrupt that balance. Hawks were also considered especially sacred birds. Small hawks would fight larger raptors to defend their nests and young. Their flight denoted great powers, as they could soar effortlessly on the wind and then dive with great speed to seize their prey and inflict instant death with their talons. It is not certain if the Missouria, Otoe, or Ioway shared these specific Osage concepts. However imagery involving woodpeckers and hawks was so widespread, it seems likely some common concepts of these birds' power were shared among different tribes.

Images of both kinds of birds appear as motifs on Mississippian ceramics, shell gorgets (medallions), and copper bas-relief panels. An Oneota-period Catlinite tablet found at the Utz site by Jim Utz in 1936 has some supernatural connotation. One side bears the image of a woodpecker, a resident of the Upper World. Markings on the bird's throat are interpreted as a speech symbol. A mace, a type of war club, is another symbol found in Mississippian art, and it overlays the woodpecker image, as does an eagle feather, which denotes

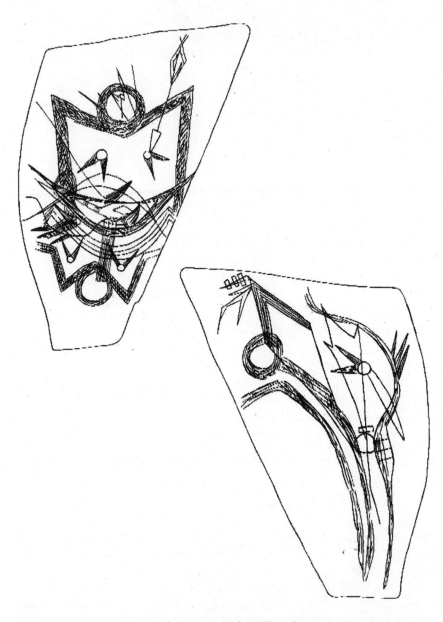

The Utz Tablet (obverse and converse sides). This Oneota tablet contains sacred design elements, some of which are similar to those found in earlier Mississippian artwork. This indicates that some similar spiritual traditions were shared among varying groups and were passed down over many generations.(Courtesy of the Missouri Department of Natural Resources)

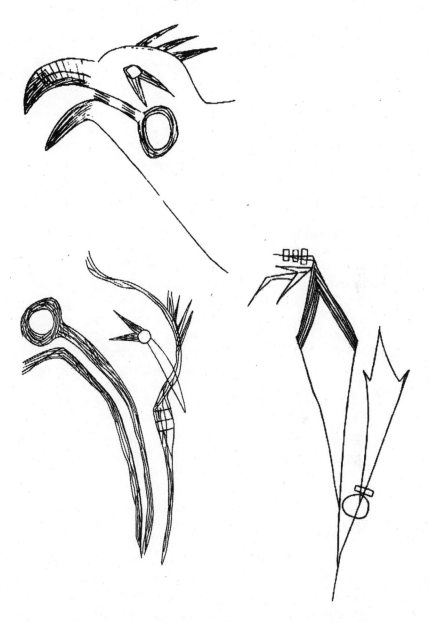

A bird of prey, probably a hawk, and a woodpecker, probably an ivorybill. The eye surround (forked eye) on the birds also appeared commonly in Mississippian art. The mace (club) and feather probably represent war honors. This imagery, shown in the Utz Tablet, was used in Otoe-Missouria, Ioway and Osage design elements. (Courtesy of the Missouri Department of Natural Resources)

a war honor. On the reverse side of the tablet are two "M"-shaped images associated with the Lower World. These are overlaid with a hawk head bearing a speech symbol. A forked eye on each bird is another symbol found in Mississippian art. The hawk may represent a Thunderer, a resident of the heavens or Upper World, which was in opposition to the Lower World. Diagonal marks on each side indicate it had been used as a cutting surface, perhaps for sacred tobacco. The tablet, which was only nine inches long, six inches wide, and half an inch thick, may have been part of a sacred bundle.

Feathers and body parts of woodpeckers and hawks and eagles were often among the ceremonial articles kept with sacred pipe bowls in the clan bundles. Hawks were an important component of the Osage war shrine and also appeared on some of their war shields. Since the Missouria were near neighbors and allies of the Osage, they may have shared similar traditions. These shrines or sacred bundles spiritually imparted the power and other qualities of the birds to the warrior. Many nineteenth-century images show Otoe-Missouria, Ioway, Omaha, Kansa, and Osage men using parts of these birds in their personal ornamentation. Headdresses often sport the mandibles of ivorybill woodpeckers, colored green with verdigris, woodpeckers' scalps, and hawks' heads and feathers. It is clear that symbolism associated with these sacred birds was widespread in Woodland, Mississippian, and Oneota cultures and continued into the historic period of the Missouria tribe.

Jean Bernard Bossu wrote that in 1756 a delegation of Missouria came to Fort Chartres in Illinois; among them was an old woman, he wrote, "who was supposed to be a magician." She wore around her "naked body" a live rattlesnake. She spoke to the snake, which seemed to understand her. The old woman finally said to it, "I see that you are bored here. Go home and I shall meet you there when I return." She put the snake down, and it crawled into the woods in the direction of Missouria territory. Bossu believed that the woman was playing some magician's trick. The Jesuit priests saw this interaction as a sign of devil worship. Putting aside the bias of the report, a closer examination of the incident provides a further glimpse into Missouria spirituality.

Communication with a snake could signify she was a member of the Snake Clan or that it was her spiritual grandfather guardian or that she was simply in communion with the "snake people." She was probably a symbolic representation of a spirit woman, called in some cultures "Old-Woman-Who-Never-Dies" or "Grandmother Earth" or simply "Grandmother." *Hin kunye,* Grandmother, was the first woman to appear after the creation of the universe. The first of her two husbands was another powerful spirit, "Old-Man-Immortal," who was symbolized by a rattlesnake or sometimes a horned serpent. In some Siouan cultures, *wakan,* snakes were associated with the Lower World, water, and agricultural fertility. The woman undoubtedly possessed sacred knowledge. Possibly she practiced healing arts as well. She likely was the person to seek for treating snakebites.

The Southern Siouans had medical societies that sometimes transcended the clan system. Members of these societies possessed special powers of healing. Europeans called them "medicine men," but they were actually *wa wehi,* healers or doctors, and might be men or women. Besides spiritual and ceremonial knowledge, they possessed knowledge of the medicinal qualities of native plants and were specialists in their fields. The Buffalo Lodge Medicine Society specialized in setting broken bones. Their medicine was said to surpass that of other medicine societies. The Red Bean Society specialized in administering purgatives. There was also a Snake and a Bear Medicine Society. Some European explorers acknowledged the success of these doctors. Truteau wrote in 1795 that among the tribes of the Missouri River, he had seen advanced cases of "rot" from some diseases completely cured by Indian doctors with "concoctions of herbs."

A ceremony widely practiced in one form or another by the Southern Siouans and other agricultural tribes was the Green Corn Ceremony, held as ears of corn began to ripen. In July of 1804, William Clark knew most Indians were hunting buffalo on the plains but thought he might find the Otoes returning to their village, "to gather the green Indian corn." It is safe to assume the early Missouria held a Green Corn Ceremony as well. The ceremony marked a new year, and it was a time to renew the sacred fire, the power of medicine bundles, to name children, and to thank Wakanda for success in the previous year's hunt and harvest. The ceremony was also a time of social unity and spiritual purification, where people could partake of the first fruits of the season, especially the growing green corn. Grandmother's help was sought to promote not only the fertility of crops but also that of the people. Corn and children were both necessary to assure the perpetuation of the tribe. Today a First Harvest celebration is held in addition to the Green Corn Ceremony.

Symbols from Mississippian cultural sites are identifiable with the historic accounts of the Green Corn Ceremony and traditions about Grandmother. Sculpted figures and images on pottery depict an old woman bearing a corn plant, and sometimes a serpent encircles her. In many cultures, it was Grandmother who had given corn to the people in the mythical times. Otoe-Missouria and Ioway tradition holds that *wadúji*, corn, came from *che*, the buffalo. There were four buffalo brothers who descended from the heavens. While on the earth, one of them died, and his brothers buried him in a buffalo wallow. When they returned to his grave the following spring they found something strange growing from his ribcage. There were stalks of corn of all colors, blue, white, red, and speckled. The vines of vegetables like squash and melon grew where his body lay. When it all had ripened, the three buffalo brothers harvested it and shared it with human beings.

Traditions of the Southern Siouans indicate a strong belief in reincarnation and resurrection of the dead. There was an afterlife in the spirit world, but sometimes individuals could come back as humans or other creatures. Bossu told the story of a French soldier who killed a snake in an Indian lodge and was threatened by the outraged owner. The angry warrior said the snake was the spirit of his deceased father. The Southern Siouan have many such stories in which Holy Spirit Beings or heroes are killed but then brought back to life through ceremonial or spiritual means. As illustrated in the story of the lost woman and the grizzly bear, sometimes the dead tried to return to their normal lives. Grandmother Earth also symbolized this resurrection process. Corn literally died when it was harvested, but when the seed was sown back into the Earth, it would regenerate, beginning the cycle of life anew.

Most Europeans and Euro-Americans viewed the Missouria and other American Indians as a simple people, without structure or purpose in their belief systems and worldview. In reality their beliefs and philosophy were sophisticated and complex and produced a strong, vibrant social order in their lives. They lacked only the ability to write this information down. Each clan carried a part of this ancient and sacred knowledge and passed it to the next generation by oral tradition. Elders watched children closely and carefully selected and groomed those few who could be entrusted with these traditions. Even though the surviving information is fragmentary, the Missouria can be seen to be a rich, active culture attuned to the cosmos and the forces of nature.

2

The Europeans Arrive

Change and Continuity

Father Gabriel Marest wrote to Louisiana's Governor Pierre Lemoyne d'Iberville on June 10, 1700, explaining that the reason the Pekitanoui River was also called the "Missouri" was because "that people are the first who are found there." Anecdotal evidence suggests the Missouria at one time had villages near the mouth of the Missouri River and locations downstream from the Utz and Gumbo Point sites. Missouria sites could have been obliterated by nature or human activity, or they may await discovery and classification. Villages were periodically moved due to warfare, tribal politics, or the need for new resources.

Early reports indicate the Missouria were extremely numerous and powerful. During exploration of the Mississippi valley in 1682, Robert LaSalle wrote that on the Missouri River were "a great number of large villages of many different nations." Nicholas LaSalle wrote, "We camped near the mouth of a river which falls into the Mississippi. It is called the river of the Missouris. The river crosses from the northwest and is thickly settled judging from what the savages say." Henri Tonty at this time reported the river was "abundantly peopled." Another report from 1698 said the "nation of the Missouris is very considerable, and has given its name to the large river that empties itself into the Mississippi." In 1702, M. de Remonville, an investor in the Company of the Mississippi, wrote that the Missouri River "is a considerable stream, upon whose banks are fourteen very numerous nations."

Some archaeologists believe that prior to European contact, the Missouria could have numbered as many as 10,000 individuals. Governor Iberville in Mobile estimated that there were "1,500 families" of Missouria in 1700. Unfortunately he does not define the family unit. Indian households were multigenerational, and often the extended family resided in the same lodge. Moreover, a Missouria man might have more than one wife, each with children.

There could have been 5 to 10 or even more people in each of Iberville's "families," or 7,500 to 16,500 people. If Iberville was counting male heads of households to define "families," that is about 1,500 able-bodied men. Early explorers estimated that 20 to 25 percent of a tribe's population was made up of able-bodied hunters and warriors. Applying this interpretation to Iberville's estimate still yields a potential Missouria population of 6,000 to 7,500 individuals.

In 1820 George Champlain Sibley, factor at Fort Osage, described the difficulty of determining the Osage population: "They are continually removing from one village to another quarrelling or intermarrying, so that the strength of no particular village can even be correctly ascertained. . . . They are always at war and not a year passes when they do not lose some that way. Epidemic diseases attack them now and then, and sweep them off by families." His statement demonstrated the difficulty of getting an accurate census of any Indian tribe; however, colonial officials made serious efforts to enumerate the members of the native nations. They needed to assess the potential for trade as well as the military capability the Indians possessed. While the exact numbers will never be known, it is clear that at the time of first contact with Europeans the Missouria were a numerous and powerful people.

Father Marc Bergier at the Tamaroa mission made a report in 1702 that departed from the tone of the previous ones. He wanted to establish missions among the Kansa and Pawnee because the Osage were "too numerous," but the Missouria he wrote, "are reduced to nothing." Some historians believe that an epidemic, probably smallpox, ravaged the Missouria at this time. Father Bergier, however, provided no other details in his report. Historians and archaeologists now believe that when the Europeans reached the North American coast, pandemics of smallpox, measles, cholera, and influenza began spreading inland along trade routes. In 1541 the Spanish army under

Spanish conquistador Hernando De Soto led an exploration of the American Southeast and the lower Mississippi valley in 1540 to 1542. Disease carried by the conquistadors proceeded ahead of the expedition and killed many Indians, severely disrupting the native cultures. (Courtesy of the State Historical Society of Missouri)

Hernando de Soto had traversed the southeastern United States and discovered the Mississippi River, eventually reaching present-day northern Arkansas and southeast Missouri. As cruel as de Soto's soldiers were to the Indian people, evidence suggests deadly disease advanced ahead of the conquistadors. De Soto had found an empty town of five hundred lodges, abandoned, his guides told him, because of a pestilence. In another town they found four lodges filled with the bodies of people killed by some unknown disease.

Imported diseases decimated some Indian tribes that would not actually see a European for decades. Systems of trade and divisions of farm labor producing a reliable food supply all collapsed, adding to the panic and chaos created by the rapidly rising death toll. Seventy-five percent or more of the New World's native population may have perished from disease. Along the lower Mississippi valley de Soto had seen numerous villages and fields of corn but had not reported seeing bison. One hundred and forty years later, La Salle described the same area as "wilderness scarcely touched by man" and abundant in "wild cattle." The logical conclusion is that the human population in that area had collapsed, and the subsequent lack of hunting had allowed bison herds to expand south and east from the western prairies.

Few reports of epidemics specifically mention the Missouria. Details about epidemics in this period are not well documented. Communications between Europe and its New World colonies were poor, and relations with the indigenous nations were in their infancy. What is clear is that the Missouria population began declining precipitously soon after European contact. Examining how epidemics affected other tribes provides insight into how the Missouria were probably affected. Father Jean St. Cosmé visited the "Acanscas" (Arkansas or Quapaw) in 1699 and "found the nation . . . formerly so numerous entirely destroyed by war and disease . . . smallpox had carried off most of them. In one village all the children had died and a great many women. Not a hundred men were left."

Smallpox, measles, influenza, and Asiatic cholera probably swept up the Missouri River valley multiple times. Europeans had a somewhat greater degree of immunity than the Indians to these diseases but still succumbed in fairly high numbers themselves. Whenever communicable disease appeared in the settlements of the Louisiana Territory or the Illinois Country, it almost certainly made its way to the villages of the Missouria and those of neighboring tribes.

Indians also contracted smallpox in the East at the close of the French and Indian War. As they returned to their homes in 1763, they carried the disease, and it spread among the population along the Missouri River, striking the Missouria and Little Osage. James Mackay, a Scotsman turned Spanish trader in St. Louis, wrote of another epidemic: "In 1781 the small pox destroyed above two thirds of the Indian Tribes of the north part of America. Many tribes in the Western Countries who were numerous when the first settlements were made on the Mississippi are now extinct and of the Kaskaskias, Peorias, Missouries, and several others are only left in a sufficiency to inform us that Tribes of that name existed in times past."

When the Missouria moved from the Pinnacles onto the flood plain at Gumbo Point, they probably increased their risk of exposure to disease from any passing infected trader or voyageur. The bottomland location also increased exposure to malaria-carrying mosquitoes in the warm months. The Pinnacles had caught the south winds coming off the prairies, keeping mosquito numbers down and reducing the chance for mosquito-borne infections.

The tribal medicine societies had learned over centuries what plants and herbs to use to treat illnesses. There was no time to learn how to cope with the new epidemics. The doctors and spiritual leaders who provided guidance in times of crisis were themselves afflicted. When they died the ability to pass down accumulated tribal history, traditions, and wisdom to younger generations was disrupted. Ritual ceremonies for the dead were abbreviated. Archaeological excavations at the Little Osage village near the Missouria village found a large number of shallow graves. Usually the Osage buried their dead in a sitting position. These graves suggest rather hasty burials, perhaps as the result of either the 1763 or 1781 smallpox epidemic.

Anthropologists previously gave very low population estimates of Indians in North America based on the reports of early American explorers and pioneers. It is now thought that those the Americans found were the remnants of once-more-numerous peoples. The early French had reported many villages and people on the Missouri River. A little over a century later, Lewis and Clark found few people but many abandoned villages along the river. Clark reported that the Arikara Nation once had 11 villages, but that only 2 remained after a smallpox epidemic in 1801. Fur trader Auguste Chouteau reported that before the 1801 epidemic the Missouria and Kansa each could field 250 warriors and the Otoe between 100 and 200 warriors. The smallpox, he said, had cut their numbers in half. In 1673, there were at least 5,000 Missouria and possibly many more. By 1777, their population had declined to around 1,000. By 1804, fewer than 400 remained, most with the Otoe but others among the Little Osage, the Kansa, and the Ioway. As the Missouria population declined, so did their ability to influence regional events and remain a viable, independent nation.

The Missouria homeland and its resources were increasingly strained as Europeans spread west of the Mississippi River. Indian nations did not recognize national boundaries in the manner of Europeans. Hunting areas overlapped, sometimes even if one tribe resented the presence of another in that territory. However, certain areas could be recognized more or less as the "home territory" for individual nations. William Clark described the Missouria territory before they joined the Otoe: "These people are the real proprietors of an extensive and fertile country lying on the Missouri (River) above their ancient village for a considerable distance, and as low as the mouth of the Osage River, and thence to the Mississippi." George Sibley in 1819 described the Grand River valley saying, "The Missouris once claimed there, but they have long since abandoned the country and left the Ioway in possession of it." Auguste Chouteau in 1801 had reported that the Missouria had hunted both banks of the Missouri from the Lamine River to the "Fire Prairie" at present-day Sibley, Missouri. An unnamed Missouria headman told government agents in 1819 that they had once inhabited the country from the mouth of the Missouri to the Rocky Mountains. His statement indicates that the Missouria periodically roamed far onto the Great Plains. Raiding and trading parties traveled even well beyond the normal hunting range. In August of 1825 an Otoe-Missouria war party raided an Arapaho camp on the Arkansas River at the base of the Rocky Mountains.

The Missouria homeland represented an ecological transition zone where eastern forests merged with western prairies. The rivers and their tributaries were a mosaic of bottomland forest, wet prairies, and marshland. Common trees included cottonwood, elm, hackberry, sycamore, silver maple, pecan, and willow. Extensive alluvial prairies occurred in the floodplain, usually on the scars of old river channels. Their rich soil, which nourished the crops grown by Missouria women, was replenished each spring as the Missouri River overflowed its banks, depositing nutrient-rich silt in the fields.

The marshlands and swamps bordering the rivers provided abundant habitat for songbirds, waterfowl, and wading birds. Among the once-flourishing species there were ivory-billed woodpeckers, trumpeter swans, sandhill cranes, ruffed grouse, passenger pigeons, bald eagles, and Carolina parakeets. The waterways teemed with fish, turtles, mussels, frogs, and aquatic mammals such as beavers, otters, minks, and muskrats. The plants of the wetlands marshes included bulrushes, horsetail, cattails, and water lilies.

The uplands were gently rolling hills covered by big bluestem prairie grass interspersed with patches of oak-hickory woodlands and savannas. *Taglóglo* (turkeys), *ta* (white-tailed deer), and *mantó thewe* (black bears), were abundant. The prairies sustained large flocks of *so-xanje* (prairie chickens) and *tó dai e wayije* (bobwhite quail), and large herds of *che* (bison) and *huma* (elk) were common. *Wapaxkówe* (mountain lions), *shú^{n}ta xóje* (gray wolves), and *udwá^n ba i* (bobcats) were the main predators in this rich natural environment. The Missouria had names, and potential uses, for every plant and animal found in this rich, diverse environment.

Lightning strikes were a common cause of fires on the Great Plains. Such natural fires were rarer on Missouri prairies as rainfall usually accompanies lightning and puts out the fires. But according to early reports, Indians frequently set fire to the prairies to signal one another or to drive game. Burning the prairies removed woody growth and promoted luxurious new growth of grass, attracting herds of bison and elk. These grazing animals further reduced woody plant growth. Hunting was easier on prairies and savannas than in thick forest or brushy undergrowth. The Missouria and their neighbors were, in effect, managing the prairies as "pasture" for their bison, deer, and elk herds.

Historically, prairie lands made up one-third of what is now Missouri. About 70 percent of what is present-day Saline County was prairie. While en route to build Fort Osage in 1808, William Clark crossed the Missouri River at the Arrow Rock bluff. He then crossed "open plains" as he headed west past the "ancient villages" of the Missouria and Little Osage. This was the beginning of the "sea of grass" that continued almost uninterrupted to the mountains. Elk and deer were there, and he saw "signs of buffalo" near the old village sites. Within another decade American settlers would exterminate the remaining bison and most of the elk in this area. Without Indians setting fire to the prairie grass and large herds of animals grazing, woody vegetation and trees encroached on the prairies. Today this region is more heavily wooded than at any time in the eighteenth and nineteenth centuries.

When documentation of Indian tribal life began in the mid-nineteenth century, the Missouria had already lost much of their distinctive culture and traditions. A fair amount of information survives about other Southern Siouans, especially the Osage, Omaha, and Ho Chunk. Once again, comparing cultural similarities of these tribes and contrasting that with the archaeological record allows us to make some reasonable assumptions about Missouria material culture.

The Southern Siouans shared a core set of themes in their social structure and spiritual beliefs, as well as in agricultural and hunting practices, which is manifested in their oral traditions. Neighboring Caddoan- and Algonquin-speaking tribes also applied many of these broad concepts. Despite the similarities, each nation developed and maintained its own unique identity. While imperceptible to most Europeans these cultural variations were readily recognizable by members of the tribes.

American Indians in the midwestern states were traditionally classified in either the Plains or the Woodland cultural group. However the Southern Siouans and many of their immediate neighbors are not easily categorized. The Osage, for example, possessed cultural traits

Mahinkacha or Maker of Knives by Karl Bodmer, 1834. This
picture was probably made at the trading post of Joseph
Roubidoux in the Blacksnake Hills, now St. Joseph, Missouri.
Spelling variations of the Roubidoux family name survive
among the Otoe-Missouria and Ioway today. Prince Maximilian described Mahinkacha as "an athletic youth." He wears
the traditional scalp lock of Missouria men and glass and
bone bead necklaces and earrings. (Courtesy of the Missouri
Department of Natural Resources)

that have been identified with the Great Plains, the Southeast Woodlands, and the Northeast Woodlands. The Missouria certainly had
the same opportunities as the Osage for diverse cultural interchange
and influences. Surrounding cultural traits met and blended in the
Midwest prairies without a single characteristic becoming predomi-
nant. As a result, these tribes are sometimes recognized today as their
own Prairie cultural group.

The typical Missouria male was similar in appearance to his Siouan
neighbors and kinsmen. Most descriptions of the Missouria's physical appearance were made in the early nineteenth century. Germany's
Maximilian, Prince of Wied, who traveled up the Missouri River in
1833, noted their dress and customs did not differ greatly from those
of the Sac Indians. "They had holes in their ears, in which they wore
bunches of wampum: some young men had red cloth tied round
their heads, and one of them wore a cap made of the entire skin of a
bear's head, with the ears, which gave him a very grotesque appearance. . . . Mr. Bodmer took the portrait of an athletic Missouri youth."
Swiss artist Karl Bodmer accompanied Maximilian and made many
striking portraits of Indians.

The men wore moccasins and knee- or thigh-length leather leggings
and a breechcloth of buckskin. In warm months they went about bare
chested. John Treat Irving Jr., in September of 1833, observed "paint
of every hue laid upon their bodies . . . their heads were decorated
with feathers and variegated plumage of the gaudy birds . . . some
wore glittering armlets and collars of tin. Their heads were shaven
and covered with vermilion [red paint]." In 1834, George Catlin, the
noted western artist, said the men cut their hair leaving "a small tuft
on the crown usually ending in a ponytail or braid." This hairstyle is
a scalp lock but today is popularly called a "Mohawk." There were
exceptions. Maximilian saw one Missouria man with hair halfway
down his back.

Women wore loose-fitting pullover dresses of deerskin, moccasins,
and sometimes leggings. It was practical dress for farming, dressing
animal hides, and other chores. Their hair was parted in the middle,
and each day a red line was painted on the part, symbolizing the path
of the sun, the giver of life. Small children were allowed to go naked
in the summer months up until puberty. Buffalo robes constituted
winter wear for everyone. Trade cloth and wool blankets sometimes
displaced native materials but still followed traditional patterns.

Clothing for ceremonial purposes was far more elaborate and decorated with feathers from various birds, paint, and quillwork. Porcupine

quills were traded throughout North America. These were flattened; cut into strips; dyed various colors using plants, berries, or minerals; and then woven into or sewn on shirts and leggings. Beads acquired from European traders were made into necklaces and earrings and later used in design elements on moccasins and ceremonial objects. In later years, decorative strips made from small "seed beads" replaced quillwork for edging and trim on clothing. The geometric and floral designs of paint, quillwork, and beadwork on clothing and buffalo robes carried spiritual significance. Because their dress was rooted in longstanding customs and spiritual traditions it is likely the appearance of the Missouria people in the early nineteenth century had changed little over the previous hundred years.

Edwin James wrote that the tribes on the Missouri River traveled to the Great Plains "to make war" on the *manto*, grizzly bear. Plains grizzlies formerly ranged the western two-thirds of present-day Kansas and Nebraska. Killing a grizzly was an especially dangerous proposition and an honor requiring great bravery. Only handheld weapons such as knives, clubs, tomahawks, or lances were allowed. The bear's claws were made into necklaces, which imparted the strength and ferocity of the bear to the wearer, indicating a formidable warrior. Sonny Littlecrow described how eagle feathers for headdresses were obtained. A warrior hid in a hole, under brush or a buffalo robe with a live rabbit tethered nearby. When an eagle landed to strike the rabbit, the warrior reached out and grabbed it by the legs.

Another form of ornament used by the Indians were tattoos. Most were reserved for people of distinction. The Missouria and many other tribes of the prairies, plains, and woodlands practiced tattooing. Otoe-Missouria elder Grace Kihega recalled in 1980 being tattooed as a little girl. She received a small blue spot in the center of her forehead, which was used for a girl's puberty, "coming of age" ceremony. Tattoos had spiritual and clan significance and were not merely for decoration, although the owners took great pride in them. Jean Bernard Bossu was adopted by the Quapaw in the 1750s and described the tattooing process, which would have been the same for the Missouria and other Southern Siouan cultures:

> A deer was tattooed on my thigh as a sign that I have been made a warrior and a chief. . . . I sat on a wildcat skin while an Indian burned some straw. He put the ashes in water and used this simple mixture to draw the deer. He then traced the drawing with

big needles pricking me till I bled. The blood mixed with the ashes of the straw formed a tattoo, which can never be removed . . . these marks multiply their achievements in war. One so tattooed without such deeds is degraded.

Bossu reported that the extremely painful process made him ill with a fever for a week. Few illustrations of Indian tattooing survive. Some early renderings and descriptions of the Fox, Illini, Osage, and Wichita indicate very elaborate body tattoo designs. A very few photographs of Osages show complete body tattooing. At the St. Louis World's Fair in 1904 a group of Osage men were bare chested at first, proudly showing their tattoos. Visitors pointed at the curious designs. That gesture is cursing to the Osage, so the men soon bought suits to hide their tattoos. The pictures of the Osages at the fair show them in modern dress, their cuffs and collars tightly buttoned. Whether Missouria body tattooing was as elaborate as that of the Osage, Illini, or Wichita is unknown.

The Missouria remained semisedentary, as they had been during the Oneota period. They occupied their villages on a seasonal basis and hunted the rest of the time. While they were not nomadic in the same sense as the Arapaho, Cheyenne, Kiowa, or Lakota Sioux of the Great Plains, they were still extremely mobile. It was not difficult for them to pack up camp and be on the move within hours or to travel long distances. Whenever the tribe moved, the women packed everything needed in *kóge*, painted, rawhide boxes called "parfleshe" by the French.

The women were responsible for the construction of the villages and the camps. There are no early records specifically describing the dwellings of the Missouria, but archaeological excavations found traces of two types of houses at the Utz site. One style was a square-to-rectangular shape, and the other was oval-to-elliptical in shape. Carl Chapman believed the rectangular houses found at Utz represented the earlier style home.

The *nahachi* (bark house) was a rectangular, gabled framework covered with slabs of bark overlaying one another. Often these were used as council or ceremonial houses. A single house excavated at Gumbo Point was the elliptical *chakiruthan* (house tied together) and designated the "prairie-mat lodge" by anthropologists (and is sometimes called a "wigwam"). Both styles of houses have been documented in use among the Otoe, Ioway, Ho Chunk, Kansa, Osage, Sac and Fox, and Kickapoo into the late nineteenth century. George

The prairie-mat lodge (sometimes called a "wigwam") is a style that was widely used among the tribes of the Midwest. (Reconstruction, Van Meter State Park, courtesy of Department of Natural Resources)

Sibley wrote a description of the Osage prairie-mat lodge that corresponds closely with the posthole arrangements of the Missouria prairie-mat lodge:

> The Osage lodges are generally constructed with upright posts, put firmly in the ground of about 20 feet in height . . . the whole of the building and sides are covered with matting made of rushes two or three feet in length and four feet in width, which are joined together and entirely exclude rain. The doors are on the sides of the building, and are generally one on each side. The fires made in holes in the center of the lodge; the smoke ascending through apertures left in the roof for the purpose. At one end of the dwelling is a raised platform, about three feet from the ground, which is covered with bear skins, and generally holds all the little choice furniture of the master, and on which repose his honorable guests. . . . They vary in length from 36 to 100 feet.

Some sources have suggested that the Missouria lived in plains-style earth lodges. No archaeological or documentary evidence of plains earth lodges in Missouri has been found. The abundance of building material, including reeds, rushes, cattails, and tree bark, in central Missouri would have made earth lodges unnecessary. The Otoe, Omaha, and Kansa frequently used earth lodges, but there was less suitable plant materials and less rainfall in their territories, making earth lodge construction more practical and often necessary. However, documentation also exists that these tribes sometimes used the bark house and the prairie-mat lodge. The Missouria probably never lived in earth lodges until after they joined the Otoe.

The Otoe, Ioway, Kansa, and Osage also used the conical skin tipi on hunting trips. The Osage mainly had hunting camps containing smaller versions of the wigwam. These base camps were set up at regular intervals along well-established hunting trails and used year after year. The Osage covered the lodge framework of each temporary abode with hides they brought along. There is no documentation of the Missouria using the plains tipi, or *chibothraje* (house stands upright), prior to joining the Otoe, although it is possible. Undoubtedly they also had established hunting camps throughout their territory.

The Missouria subsisted by hunting more than by agriculture. From approximately mid-March to mid-May they stayed in their villages preparing for spring planting. Then they went on the summer bison hunt, returning to the village from mid-August to mid-October to harvest the crops and prepare them for winter storage. They left for another bison hunt in the fall, returning to the villages by mid-November. From late November through early March they dispersed into smaller clan groups primarily hunting deer, elk, and bear, but also bison when they found them. After the fur trade with Europeans began, smaller fur-bearing animals like beaver, otter, muskrat, fox, bobcat, and raccoon were taken in the winter hunts. This seasonal cycle of life meant that much of the year the main villages of the Missouria were virtually empty.

The women were skilled agriculturalists, growing crops of corn, beans, squash, melons, and pumpkins in the rich alluvial prairies. They crossbred plants to produce hybrids with desired characteristics, including several varieties of corn. They even had popcorn. Corn, more properly called maize, was the single most important crop of the Missouria. It was eaten fresh, put in soups, and when dry pounded into meal. Dried corn was easy to store in deep dry cache pits and was an important food source during the lean winter months. This was supplemented by dried pumpkin and squash. Europeans probably imported watermelons to the New World from Africa in the 1500s, and the seeds were quickly traded from tribe to

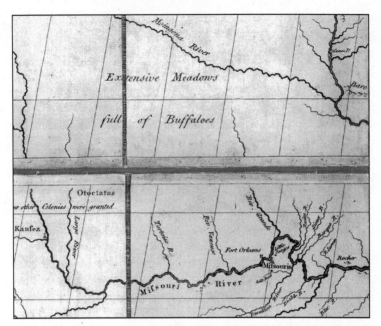

Detail from "Map of the British and French Dominions in North America" by John Mitchell of London, England, 1755. This map indicates that southern Iowa and northern Missouri was a rich buffalo range. The "Moingona River" is the Des Moines, and the "Riv. Grande" is the Grand River. The Missouria and Little Osage villages, shown in the bottom right corner, had close access to this range. (Courtesy of the David Rumsey Map Collection)

tribe. Watermelon seeds have been found in refuse pits of the Utz site predating the arrival of the French.

The women and children gathered walnuts, hickory nuts, hazelnuts, pecans, chestnuts, acorns, wild grapes, plums, papaws, blackberries, strawberries, persimmons, wild potatoes, and cattail roots. The Osage, and probably the Missouria, made a soup that used acorns and buffalo grease. (The acorns were first pounded and leached in boiling water to remove the bitter tannic acid.) Seeds from water lilies have also been found in refuse pits of archaeological sites. The women and children waded the shallow backwaters and sloughs of the Missouri River to gather these starchy tubers, which were dried, pounded into flour, and made into a kind of bread.

Weather conditions affected the abundance of wildlife and edible plants. For example, a late frost can be devastating to a nut crop, which in turn affects populations of turkey and larger animals like deer and bear. Drought could result in a poor corn crop and also affect the migration of bison and other wildlife. Warfare could disrupt the hunting cycle. These types of calamities periodically affected the Missouria and their neighbors. To ensure success in hunting, gathering, and farming, elaborate ceremonies marked each seasonal cycle and regulated activities to assure harmony with the universe. These ceremonies beseeched Wakanda, the Creator, to take pity on the people and help them. The Missouria knew that the failure of any hunt or crop could bring disaster.

Bison, more commonly called "buffalo," were a vital commodity to tribes on the Midwest's prairies and Great Plains, as early European explorers often mentioned. Father Marquette and Father Louis Hennepin wrote of the Illini hunting bison on foot in central Illinois. Henri Tonty wrote in 1684 that along the Missouri River were the "Ajooija" (Ioway), "Ototenta" (Otoe), and "Emissourita" (Missouria), "where the buffaloes which are found everywhere in Louisiana comes from." Explorer Jean Baptiste de La Harpe wrote in 1719 that the Osage and Missouria stayed in their villages in the spring "and pass the winter in chasing the buffalo, which are very abundant in these parts." A Spanish report from 1767 proposed that a garrison at the mouth of the Missouri River could subsist on the abundant "wild cattle" found there. Truteau wrote in 1795 that along the Missouri River "there are large low prairies on which one generally sees herds of the wild cattle which pasture there."

The Missouria often hunted between the Grand River and the Des Moines. A map drawn by English botanist John Mitchell in 1755 identifies this region as "Extensive Meadows Full of Buffaloes." For the next forty years mapmakers continue to identify this area of lush, nutritious, tallgrass prairie as "Immense Prairie full of Buffalo," "Buffaloes Meadows," or "Extensive meadows full of Buffaloes, Elks and Deers." Even as late as 1833 Maximilian wrote that at the headwaters of the Grand River, "buffaloes, elks and stags were still reported to be numerous." It was a simple matter for the Missouria to cross the Missouri River and follow the Grand into this rich buffalo range.

Individual bison herds on the Great Plains contained thousands of animals, sometimes tens of thousands. Herds on the Midwest's prairies seem to have been more scattered and ranged in size from a few dozen to several hundred animals. Their smaller size would have made hunting easier for the Missouria. Such herds could be more easily surrounded or driven toward waiting hunters without spooking other nearby herds. Several hundred stampeding bison were easier to evade than several thousand. Europeans noted their predilection for hunting and concluded that Indian men were lazy. However, bison, elk, and bear were not hunted for sport though there was a recreational component to it. It was dangerous business, but necessary for the survival of the tribe.

Near the Gumbo Point site in 1833, Maximilian recorded a small stream called "Bonnet de Bouef," or Buffalo Hat. He wrote that the name came from "the caps, with ox horns, which the Indians who formerly dwelt here, wore in their dances." To ensure success of the bison hunts, dancers would imitate the buffalo and the hunters pursuing them. No doubt, the Missouria conducted these ceremonials prior to their bison hunts, followed by a thanksgiving ceremonial after each successful hunt.

There is an unusual rock formation on the Missouri River just west of present-day Jefferson City. Lewis and Clark called this formation Mine Hill in 1804; later it became known as Sugar Loaf Rock. In the 1830s, John Dougherty, agent for the Pawnee, Ioway, Otoe, and Missouria, told Maximilian "that the Ioways said this was the petrified dung created by a race of heavenly bison." The buffalo was an animal of the Sky division. The Missouria undoubtedly observed this tradition about the rock formation since this was their home territory before the arrival of the Ioway. Because the buffalo had come to earth at this spot it was probably a sacred place. Modern Euro-Americans would recoil at the notion of a place associated with dung being considered sacred. Henri Tonty in 1684 had explained that the Missouria, Otoe, and Ioway "almost exclusively" used the dried dung of bison for fuel for their fires. It burned without odor and discouraged the presence of mosquitoes. It exemplifies how the Indians utilized every part of the natural environment for survival.

Oneota and Missouria trash pits contain abundant remains of deer, black bear, turkey, and a wide variety of waterfowl, birds, turtles, fish, frogs, and smaller mammals, like raccoons and skunks. All these animals were sources of protein. Bison and elk remains are relatively rare in trash pits, except for the bison scapula used to make hoes for farming. The lack of bison bone material at archaeological sites and the rare mention of bison by American explorers have led some to conclude that the animals were always rare in Missouri. Hunting parties brought meat and hides back to the villages, but the size and weight of the bones would have made transporting them difficult. And the Missouria had no need for them as their marrow could be extracted at the campsite. Early French and Spanish reports indicate that bison were common on the prairies of western and northern Missouri. Clearly bison were an important component of Missouria culture. However, these herds were depleted as European settlements on the Mississippi River grew. The Indians traded hides and supplied meat to the posts of the Illinois Country. European hunters ventured out from the settlements to hunt as well. By the time Americans arrived in 1804, bison had been overhunted in much of Missouri.

Societies change constantly to adapt to changing environmental conditions or to take advantage of new opportunities. Missouria society underwent a dramatic technological transformation with the arrival of European trade goods. Stone and bone tools gave way to those made of metal. The metal tools offered advantages. An example is the difference between a stone and steel axe. For the former, a skilled craftsman had to find hard granite or rhyolite stones of approximately the right size and weight and then undertake the painstaking labor to shape them. A metal axe was easier to sharpen and couldn't break or chip as easily as stone. Wood could be chopped more efficiently and quickly. Metal also made a lighter weapon, easier to carry in battle. Extra pelts taken during a hunt could be traded for these labor-saving, seemingly miraculous items.

Missouria cultural transformation accelerated as the number of French traders increased, first in the Mississippi valley and then on the Missouri River itself. However, this transformation was made in the context of the Missouria worldview. The Missouria did not use every European trade item as it was designed or intended. Metal pots and kettles were sometimes broken up and made into arrowheads. Gun barrels, if broken or worn out, were converted into hide scrapers or other tools. Guns became the single most important commodity of the fur trade, but bows and arrows were never completely abandoned. When the Missouria acquired cloth and wool blankets the materials were cut and adapted to their fashion. Items made of native materials were never completely abandoned. Animal hides still provided much of the material for clothing, especially moccasins and leggings and sometimes coverings for the lodges. Stone tools or arrow points were still occasionally made, and others were recycled and kept in use. Missouria women still made and used clay pots for cooking and for hauling water. They had learned that cooking in unlined copper and brass pots could taint food and cause sickness.

The Missouria and other tribes were independent nations acting in what they deemed to be their best interest; however, the growing dependence on trade goods profoundly reduced the ability of the

Indians to remain fully self-sufficient and independent. Since they could not manufacture or repair these items themselves, trade eventually became a necessity and a tool that Europeans could exploit to manipulate the Indian tribes.

The introduction of horses also had a profound impact on the culture of the prairie tribes. Horses were brought into the Great Plains by the Spanish conquistadors, starting in the 1500s. Escaped horses found the vast grasslands to their liking, and the population of wild horses exploded and spread quickly toward the east. The horse gave the Indians greater mobility and enhanced their ability to hunt the bison. Henri Tonty reported as early as 1682 that the "villages of savages" on the Missouri River "make use of horses to go to war and to carry the meat of the wild cattle which they kill."

No evidence of horses has been found at the Utz site, although the Missouria probably had them the last twenty-five years or so they resided there. Most of the Utz site has not been excavated, and if horses were still fairly rare at this time, the remains may simply not have been found. A large contingent of French traders at Cahokia in June of 1723 did accompany a group Missouria to their village "to trade in horses and buy skins." A Spanish report dated 1768 stated that the Missouria raised an abundance of horses, and the Spanish

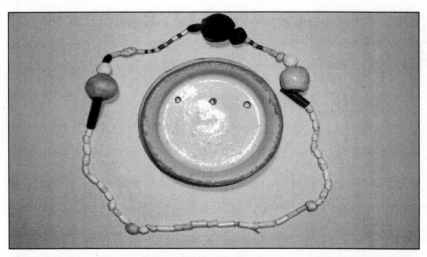

This is not a necklace but an assortment of beads salvaged from the Gumbo Point village site (ca. 1719 – 1790) in the 1930s. The gorget was worn on the neck like a medallion. This one was made from the base of a saucer, showing that the Missouria adapted trade goods to fit their culture. (Courtesy of the Missouri Department of Natural Resources)

government tried in vain to regulate the number of horses the tribe possessed. Clay effigies of horses and some horse bones have been unearthed at the later Gumbo Point village site. To sell a horse, the Missouria wanted "three guns, copper of the value of a gun, and an assortment of powder, balls, vermilion and beaker, of more than 400 livres." A "beaker" was probably a jar of beads, and the livre was an ancient French monetary unit. However up until 1720, the French were reluctant to pay the Missouria more than 140 livres' worth of merchandise for a horse. While translating the value of colonial French livres into present-day currency is difficult, we can see the purchasing power of livres at the time. A cow was worth about 30 livres; a pig, 6; and a small farm with buildings was about 1,200 livres.

Their love of horses led the Missouria to stage many horse-stealing raids against their Indian neighbors and European settlers. Spanish Governor Esteban Rodriguez Miro in 1785 stated the Missouria and Little Osage measured their wealth by the number of horses they possessed and many of these were acquired from the "Layatannes or wandering Apaches" to the west. Generosity was a valued trait among the Indians, and a man that would give horses to those in need was highly esteemed in the tribe. The best warriors and hunters always owned the most horses. There was a practical side to owning many horses. When a favorite horse was tired or injured, its owner had a ready supply of other mounts. Especially fleet animals with certain qualities were used exclusively for war, others for hunting, and still others as pack animals.

Stealing an enemy's horse was an act of bravery and a way for young men to attain status as warriors. In December of 1751, a group of Missouria found an Osage alone with some horses, killed him, and took the horses. This incident may have been a case of mistaken identity but more likely was the result of overriding lust by a group of young men to possess the horses and obtain a war honor. The repercussions from this action could have been disastrous for the Missouria if their powerful Osage neighbors had taken revenge. However, they quickly made amends to the Osages by "paying for the blood." This was an Indian custom to make amends for murder, thus preventing retaliation or all-out warfare. The offending party sent presents of horses, blankets, knives, beads, and mirrors to the relatives of the victim to "pay" for the death. Had it not been for this practice, intertribal warfare and loss of life would undoubtedly have been much greater.

The Missouria were closely allied to the Little Osage. The Osage were divided into two groups based on an ancient flood tradition. Several bands fled to the tops of the hills or the bluffs, and collectively these bands were called *Pahatsi,* Dwellers on the Hilltop. One group remained on a high terrace below the peak and was the *Udseta,* Dwellers Below. The French misinterpreted the sign-language meanings of Hilltop and Below, rendering them as "Big" and "Little" Osage. Both groups had their own headmen and acted independently of each other but maintained close ties, especially in matters of defense.

The Missouria and Little Osage made a formal peace in 1693. Afterward, colonial documents almost always mention the two tribes acting in concert. Prior to that peace they had periodically clashed. The Big Osage seemed to merely tolerate the Missouria and even occasionally threatened them. The Missouria maintained close ties with their Otoe kinsmen, but the Otoe were enemies of both the Big and Little Osage.

Alliances between Indian nations were not necessarily based on similarities of language or culture. The Ioway allied themselves with the Algonquin-speaking Sac and Fox against the Osage and sometimes their Missouria kinsmen, but they maintained close relations with the Otoe, who, of course, were close to the Missouria. Another close ally of the Missouria was the Kansa. A splinter of the Osage Nation, the Kansa occasionally fought with their Osage kinsmen until they made a lasting peace in 1806. The Missouria and Big and Little Osage were allies of the Algonquin-speaking Illini, who were enemies of the Sac and Fox. Some Illini groups joined the Osage to escape Iroquois aggression from the east. According to Pawnee scholar George Hyde, the traditions of the Missouria and other Chiwere tribes indicate early contact and friendship with the Pawnee, especially the *Skidi,* "Wolf" Pawnees. Yet all the Pawnee were implacable enemies of the Little Osage and the Kansa. Intertribal relationships were as complex as those among European nations and frequently changed to meet new situations.

European and later American officials who attempted to control Indian tribes were often frustrated by these complex intertribal relationships. Government actions sometimes caused age-old Indian alliances to fall apart and new ones to arise. Tribes often made peace or went to war irrespective of the demands of government officials. Ceremonial acts such as smoking the pipe had a stronger, more bind-ing effect on the Indian tribes than did signing a piece of paper or listening to the chiding of some government bureaucrat.

Several stories have emerged about the early history of the Missouria and their relations with other tribes. Louis Armand de Baron La Hontan was stationed at Green Bay, in present-day Wisconsin, in 1688 and did some exploration of the upper Mississippi valley. He claimed to have ascended the Missouri River from its mouth to the village of the Missourias in March of 1689 with a contingent of Fox Indians. La Hontan wrote that in four days of paddling from the Mississippi, they reached the first village of the Missouria "where I only stopped to make the people some presents that procured me a hundred turkeys, with which that people are wonderfully well stocked. After that we rowed hard against the stream and landed the next night near the second village." He sent a detachment of ten soldiers to visit this second Missouria village. The Fox wanted to attack and burn the village, but La Hontan refused. Later they reached an Osage village that he first evacuated then burned to placate his Fox allies. Other explorers familiar with Louisiana noted errors and embellishments in many of La Hontan's reports; consequently, most modern scholars do not accept him as a reliable source.

Portage des Sioux is the narrow peninsula of land between the Missouri and Mississippi rivers north of St. Louis. A small settlement was established there in 1799, and several stories have been given to account for the name. One says Dakota Sioux Indians came down the Missouri River in canoes, and Missouria warriors waited at the mouth of the river to ambush them. The Sioux discerned the trap and left the river, portaging (carrying) their canoes overland to the Mississippi River, where they safely embarked for their homeland. A second story says the Missouria were pursuing the Sioux down the Missouri River. While hidden by a bend in the river, the Sioux began portaging their canoes overland to the Mississippi River. The Missouria canoes raced by, continuing the chase. The Sioux had time to reach the safety of the Mississippi before the Missouria discovered their mistake.

A third story says the Missouria were encamped along the Missouri River about twenty-five miles above St. Louis. Scouts learned that a party of Sioux raiders was coming down the Mississippi, "looting and burning as they went." Following a council of war, the Missourias decided to ambush the Sioux at the mouth of the Missouri. As the warriors waited, the Sioux portaged their canoes across the peninsula to the Missouri River. Seeing canoes coming upstream, the Missouria women and children thought it was their own returning warriors. They discovered their error too late, and the Sioux wiped out the defenseless village. The Sioux then descended downstream and surprised the Missouria warriors from behind. In a furious battle that lasted for hours so few Missourias escaped that they were never again regarded as a nation.

Antoine LePage du Pratz, a Dutchman who lived in Louisiana, claimed to have met an old Yazoo Indian named "Monchact-Ap" who, following the death of his wife and children, wandered extensively for eight years. He followed the north bank of the Missouri River until he reached the village of the Missouria. He stayed with them to "learn their language which is spoken or understood by a great many nations." Monchact-Ap described "large meadows . . . covered with wild cattle' and said the Missouria "seldom eat anything but their flesh; they cultivate as much maize as may serve for a change." Some aspects of the du Pratz and La Hontan accounts seem plausible, but others seem to be the product of fertile imaginations, as are the conflicting stories about the naming of Portage des Sioux.

3

Early French
and Spanish Contacts

Robert de la Salle traveled to the mouth of the Mississippi in 1682, and claimed the river's drainage area for France, naming the territory "Louisiana" in honor of King Louis XIV. La Salle later established Fort St. Louis near Starved Rock on the Illinois River. The Illini, Shawnee, and others tribes settled nearby. But the Iroquois attacked the Miami, and they fled the area. La Salle feared the Iroquois would prevent the "Emissourites" (Missouria) from joining his outpost, stifling French efforts to forge an alliance with them. When the Iroquois left, a large group of Missouria and Piankeshaw joined the Fort St. Louis settlement, creating a village of "from two to three hundred fires [lodges]." The Missouria hoped to get the wondrous new trade goods brought by the Frenchmen that would make their lives easier.

No one knows when the Missouria first met Europeans. La Salle was given a young Padouca captive in 1683. The boy had been captured by Pawnees, traded to the Osage, then to the Missouria, and finally to the Illini, who gave him to La Salle. The boy told La Salle that while in a Missouria village he had seen two Frenchmen captured on the Mississippi River. One blew up a hand grenade in the presence of the Indians, telling them he would "burn the villages of their enemies with similar ones if they preserved his life and his companion." The

René Robert Cavelier, Sieur de la Salle claimed the drainage of the Mississippi River for France in 1682. The Missouria were among the many Indian nations he sought to establish trade and military alliances with. (Courtesy of the State Historical Society of Missouri)

boy witnessed him explode a second grenade directly in the village. A grenade was a hollow steel ball filled with gunpowder with a fuse inserted in it. La Salle had carried grenades during his explorations, so he knew these were two of his men.

No Missouria account of these first meetings with Frenchmen has survived. John Joseph Mathews, an Osage historian, said there was a vague Osage tribal memory of meeting Europeans, and the Missouria played a role in this tradition. Two white men came up the river with two Missouria warriors. The men wore buckskin shirts like the eastern Indians and the leggings and moccasins of the Missouria. The Osages thought these white men were hairy like bears. Their eyes and mouths were almost hidden by hair, and they even had hair on the backs of their hands. In contrast, the Missouria and Osage had very little body hair. Dried sweat and armpit odor trapped in heavy clothing was new and strange, and it sickened them.

Some hunters of the *Udseta*, or Little Osage, visiting the Missouria, had seen these men. They scowled and kept their distance from them. The pale men gave the Missouria women a mysterious thing called steel. It made it easy for the women to cut and scrape the flesh from animal hides. Some of the Missouria women eagerly attached themselves to the white men and their miraculous new implement.

The Missouria men acted as interpreters for the white men and asked to see the *Tzi Sho Kihega*, the Sky Chief, who presided in civil affairs. Members of the Osage Bear and Panther clans thought of killing the men before they reached the sanctuary of the Grand *Tzi Sho* lodge. They wet their fingers and pointed at them, a sign of death. Out of curiosity or perhaps respect for their Missouria allies, however, they left the white men alone. The men later visited with the *Hunkah Kihega*, or Earth Chief, who presided in military matters. Neither chief was impressed and called these men *I^{n}shta hi^{n}* (meaning "Heavy Eyebrows"). It was a common name, one without honor. What the Missouria first called these Frenchmen is unknown. In later years they were simply *Máu^{n}ke*, white people.

Mathews reported another fragment of Osage oral tradition concerning the Missouria. The Osage said a number of misfortunes weakened the medicine of the Missouria. They would not kill the Heavy Eyebrows and allowed each trader, trapper, or wandering vagrant to live with them and share their women. Soon what the Osage called *weluschka*, "little mystery people," living inside the Heavy Eyebrows, began killing many Missouria. About the same time the *Thá ke*, the Sac Indians, started coming to the Missouri River, attacking the Missouria. The Osage said this was why the Missouria allied themselves so strongly with the Little Osage and Kansa.

The Missouria did seem to embrace the white men coming among them readily. The Osage remained more aloof, perhaps occasionally sparing themselves from some of the disease epidemics spread by the Europeans and by those who had early contact with them, but the Missouria suffered intensely. One hundred years after meeting Europeans, the Osage remained a powerful nation and a military force to be reckoned with, while the Missouria were struggling for survival.

Catholic Jesuit priests, called "Black Robes" by the Indians, had established their missions in the Illinois Country among the tribes of the Illini confederacy, the Peoria, Kaskaskia, Cahokia, Mitchigamea, Moingwena, and Tamaroa tribes. The missions also became trade centers. European goods were bartered for the fur harvest of the Indians. The French in the Illinois Country anticipated in 1693 "great profits that would derive from the trade with the Missouries" as they were such "a numerous people."

However, a war broke out between the Missouria and the Osage, retarding trade activities. The Missouria allied with the Illini and captured some Osages to trade to the French as slaves. Father Jacques Gravier wrote in May of 1693:

> The deputies of the savages of this village, [Illini] accompanied by two Frenchmen went to seek an alliance of the Missouris and of the Osages. These French merchants with the view of carrying on advantageous trade with these tribes, made some proposals of peace to them; to these they agreed solely out of complaisance to the French, through consideration for whom they became reconciled to the Osages.

The French made it clear to the warring tribes that only through peace would they be able to get the guns, knives, hatchets, blankets, and beads they now valued. Around June 20, the deputation returned with two Osage and two Missouria headmen, "accompanied by some elders and some women." The Missouria, Osage, and Illini then made a peace that, although occasionally strained, lasted for nearly a century.

The Jesuits made some odd observations about their newfound allies. Father Gravier thought that the Missouria and Osage were not as quick-witted as the Illini and that their language was not very difficult, implying that they were a simpler people. He said the Missouria did not open their lips to speak and "the Osage speak still more from the throat than they." He had failed to consider that the Missouria and Osage were simply being cautious and reserved around these strange new Black Robes. The Illini had been acquainted with the priests much longer, leading to a livelier, less formal relationship.

Father Jean St. Cosmé was the last European known to have visited the Missouri River country in the seventeenth century. Unfortunately, he left no details of that visit. He opened a mission at the Tamaroa village in 1698. A large portion of the Missouria tribe came

Missouria women were a key component of the fur trade industry. They dressed and prepared the hides for shipping to trade centers such as Kaskaskia, Illinois, or New Orleans. The Company of the Indies dispatched agents to various Indian nations in 1701, to organize the trade in a systematic way. (Drawing from Carl H. and Eleanor F. Chapman, *Indians and Archaeology of Missouri*, revised edition, courtesy of the State Historical Society of Missouri and Stephen Chapman)

and settled at his mission along with the Peoria Illini; however, the Missouria were there not to receive spiritual enlightenment from the Father but to trade. The French settlements on the Mississippi River became the focal point of the fur trade, though the English to the southeast attempted to undermine the French by drawing the fur trade in that direction.

To counter this move, the Company of the West was formed in 1701 to bring organization to the fur trade in Louisiana. Agents of the company were ordered to "instruct the Savages regarding the best sorts of peltries and the method of preparing them." A significant change occurred in the Missouria's hunting patterns. They started systematically hunting fur-bearing animals they previously might have taken only to provide skins for ceremonial objects. In winter furs were prime, and this winter hunt for peltries was integrated into the hunting, gathering, and planting cycle that they had followed for untold generations. Women played an important role in preparing and packing animal hides for trade. Even though European trade had changed Missouria culture, they still framed this change within the context of their traditions.

Father De Gannes reported in 1705 that the "Oosages and Missourits" were coming to the Illini villages to trade for hatchets, knives, awls and other items and "are very glad to stay on the good side of that [Illini] nation." A Missouria woman told De Gannes that by following the Missouri River, crossing several lakes, and then following other rivers, one could reach the "Western Sea." The Missouria were honest in their reports but did not have firsthand knowledge of the entire route. One hundred years before Lewis and Clark set out on their so-called Voyage of Discovery to find a route to the Pacific Ocean, France was obsessed with that same goal, and the French obsession was fueled by Missouria reports. The remoteness of New France from the seat of government in Paris, however, hindered any serious full-scale exploration of the western territory.

The French wanted to establish peace among the various Indian nations of the Illinois Country and Louisiana Territory. Peace would ensure uninterrupted commerce throughout the vast territories of New France and open the way for a route to the Spanish silver mines of New Mexico. France's desire to reach the silver mines lasted for the duration of their occupation of North America. The French erroneously believed that following the Missouri River would bring them to the Spanish mines as well as to the Pacific Ocean. Early French policy toward the Indians on the Missouri River was influenced by the goal of reaching New Mexico. Decades later, when the Spanish assumed control of Louisiana Territory, they, too, believed that the Missouri River was a potential route to reach their New Mexico colonies from the Mississippi valley.

The Company of the West failed to significantly advance development of the Louisiana Territory. In 1719, the French government gave a charter or contract to the Company of the Indies to develop the territory's resources. John Law, a Scotsman working for the company, commissioned Bernard LaHarpe to lead an exploratory expedition up the Red River in 1719. While camped at a Touacara (Tawakoni) village in present-day eastern Oklahoma, LaHarpe held a council with several Caddoan-speaking tribes and learned these people suffered constantly from Missouria and Osage horse-stealing raids.

During the early period of French exploration, the Osage were expanding their area of domination to gain a larger share of the fur trade with the French. The Missouria, owing to their close alliance with the Little Osage, played a role in this expansion. The Osage and the Missouria were pushing the Caddoan and Pawnee tribes out of present-day Arkansas, Oklahoma, and Kansas. The Caddo tribes and the Wichita were eventually pushed south to the Red River, and the Pawnees were pushed north to the Republican and Platte Rivers. The Padouca, or Plains Apache, were pushed west toward the Rocky Mountains. The Comanche eventually moved into the former domain of the Padouca, causing them to be sometimes erroneously identified as "Padouca."

Numerous sources document the Osage hunting territory at its peak as bordering the Mississippi River on the east, the Arkansas and Cimarron Rivers in the south, the Missouri and Kansas River on the north, and the hundredth parallel on the Great Plains. Osage war parties ranged to the foothills of the Rocky Mountains and into central Wisconsin. The Missouria evidently accompanied the Osage in some of these expeditions. In the late 1700s, Spanish authorities in the trade center of present-day Natchitoches, Louisiana, periodically complained about Osage and Missouria raids disrupting their trade with the Caddoan tribes on the Red River.

Charles Claude du Tisné led an organized expedition from Canada to explore the Missouri River and establish trade relations with the tribes inhabiting its banks, hoping to reach the headwaters of the Rio Grande in New Mexico. The Missouria met Du Tisné near their village in 1719 and blocked his attempts to proceed upriver. Du Tisné did not indicate when his expedition started, but the fact that the Missouria were in their village in sufficient numbers to stop him indicates it was probably in May before the tribe's summer buffalo hunt.

Du Tisné threatened the Missouria, saying that the French would cut off their trade if he could not proceed. The Missouria were unimpressed and apparently were still numerous enough to easily resist French demands. Du Tisné wrote that the Missouria were "jealous" of other Indian nations upriver. As the first nation encountered by anyone ascending the Missouri River they were the natural "gatekeepers." They knew the French ultimately would have to concede. The Missouria probably saw an opportunity to become "middlemen" for the French traders, which could enhance their status among neighboring tribes.

The river systems were corridors of travel for the Indians, French, Spanish, English, and, later, the Americans. The Missouria and the Little Osage were strategically situated to control trade on the Missouri River. By 1740 they had extended that control to the Arkansas and Red rivers. They frequently stopped traders attempting to pass beyond their territory. They might rob a trader of his goods, and possibly kill an *engagé* (laborer) in the trading party. They would whip the traders with willow switches but allow them to return to the settlements alive. The message being sent to the Europeans was "You can bring your goods here and trade with us but [with] no one else."

The trade in firearms shifted the balance of power, and guns were the most highly sought-after prizes of the entire fur trade. Those Indian nations who were armed with guns could dominate those who were not. Some Illini Indians told the French that the Meskwaki (Fox) had waited near the Missouria village to ambush Du Tisné but had withdrawn when they realized soldiers were in his party. The Fox did not want the French reaching the Missouria and trading guns to them anymore than the Missouria wanted them trading guns to tribes farther upriver.

The Missouria had no intention of being passive participants in trade with the Europeans. Stopping traders on the Missouri River became a common practice for them and for the Little Osage. The Missouria have been described by some sources as being especially subservient to the French. However, the tribe dealt with the French on their own terms and within the context of their culture. When the Missouria could benefit from French objectives they were loyal allies and trading partners, but they did not tolerate abuse. Bossu reported that in these early times a French trader cheated the Missouria out of their furs by telling them to plant their gunpowder so they could harvest more. He sold his stock of gunpowder to them and while they were waiting for "the harvest," he retreated to Illinois. When the "harvest failed to occur the Missouria swore vengeance on the next Frenchman they caught." The trader's partner arrived in the village and quickly had his merchandise confiscated. When the trader complained about payment, the Indians told him they would pay him as soon as they harvested their gunpowder.

In the 1670s, warfare in the Great Lakes region between the Iroquois, Five Nations, and the Algonquin tribes had set off a chain reaction of tribal migrations. Beaver was already being depleted in the Great Lakes. English and French competition for the fur trade ignited the war, and the introduction of firearms took intertribal warfare to a new level. Refugee tribes, fleeing Iroquois expansion, crowded into present-day Wisconsin. By 1700 groups of the Sac and Fox nations were wandering onto the prairies of Illinois, Missouri, and Iowa. The Sac and Fox soon acquired horses and adapted to hunting bison, but competition for hunting grounds repeatedly brought them into sharp conflict with the allied Missouria, Osage, and Illini.

The Fox in particular sought to position themselves as trade middlemen between the French and other native nations. When the Fox attempted to ally with the powerful Dakota Sioux in Minnesota, the French position in Illinois was threatened. The result was a series of wars between France and its Indian allies and the Fox and their allies, the Mascouten and Kickapoo.

In 1712, the Fox alliance besieged Fort Pontchartrain at Detroit, Michigan. France called on its Indian allies to relieve the fort. Commander Jacques Duboisson reported seeing "the army of the nations of the south" issuing from the forest. All of the warriors of the Missouria tribe were present and "accompanied in the usual Indian fashion by their women, children and dogs." The Osage and Illini were also present. The siege was broken, and the Fox and the Mascouten received a beating from the Missouria and their allies while the Kickapoo managed to escape the blow. Quiet and order were temporarily restored in the Illinois Country. However, the battle initiated a blood feud between the Fox and Missouria, which would culminate in disaster for the Missouria nearly eighty years later.

Assigned to Fort Pontchartrain at the time was Ensign Etienne Vienard Sieur de Bourgmont, who was to become an important figure to the Missouria. Legend has it that following the battle of Detroit, Bourgmont fell in love with the young daughter of a Missouria headman. It is certain that when the Missouria returned home Ensign

Bourgmont deserted his post and accompanied them. He married the Missouria girl by their custom and, in 1714, had a son with her. Popular legend calls this woman the "Missouri Princess." However the term *princess* expressed an entirely European concept; it did not exist in Southern Siouan cultures. She was the daughter of a headman but was probably his second or even his third daughter. The position of eldest daughter was one of honor; she would be saved for a worthy man from within the tribe and not allowed to marry outsiders.

Bourgmont is the first Frenchman who visited the Missouria whose name is known to history. While living with them he made several explorations up the Missouri River. His experiences helped forge a close relationship between the French and the Missouria. In the spring of 1713, Bourgmont and a companion named Bourdon with a party of Missouria traveled to the capital of Louisiana, then located at Mobile, Alabama.

Bourgmont's abandonment of Detroit and his lifestyle among the Missouria were viewed as "scandalous, even criminal" by the Catholic Church. Father Pierre Tellier, the archbishop of Reims and personal priest to King Louis XIV, ordered his arrest. The orders were never carried out, and by 1714, Bourgmont was back in the Missouria village beyond the reach of Church authorities. During this return trip, Bourgmont kept a log from which Guillaume DeLisle drew the first accurate map of the lower Missouri River. Unfortunately, Bourgmont's document was strictly a navigational log and tells us little about the Missouria people.

France's interest in Louisiana grew, as reports of its agricultural, mineral, and fur resources became known. Bourgmont's knowledge of the country and his relationship with the Missouria Nation was strategically important to the colonial government. This is probably why Governor La Mothe Cadillac never acted on the orders to arrest Bourgmont. The new governor, General Jean-Baptiste Le Moyne de Bienville, was even open about supporting Bourgmont, and on September 25, 1718, he recommended that the explorer be given the Cross of St. Louis, France's highest decoration. Bourgmont took headmen of the Missouria, Illini, and Osage to Dauphin Island in Mobile Bay to counsel with Bienville in 1719. They smoked the Sacred Pipe together as a sign of allegiance.

Bourgmont returned to France in the summer of 1720, where he was hailed as a hero. Accompanying him was his six-year-old half-Missouria son, who was a novel attraction in the French court. The

Introduced by Europeans, horses transformed Missouria culture. The Indians gained increased mobility, and horses became items of trade and prizes of war. The travois, seen here lashed to a horse, enabled more efficient transport of large amounts of camp gear, animal hides, and trade goods. (Courtesy of the State Historical Society of Missouri)

king awarded Bourgmont the Cross of St. Louis and made him "Commandant of the Missouri River." With his new authority and financing through the Company of the Indies, Bourgmont proposed heading an expedition into the interior of Louisiana to make peace with the Padouca Nation [Plains Apache] and reach the Spanish mines at Santa Fe and the "Sea of the West."

The increased activity of the French in the Missouri valley alarmed Spain. The Spanish knew if the French reached Santa Fe or the Pacific Ocean it could spell the end of their empire in North America. French traders who slipped guns past the Missouria and Osage traded them to the plains tribes. The Pawnee and Wichita were trading for horses from the Spanish. If they had a reliable supply of French guns, they would have no incentive to trade and could then threaten Spanish interests. Spain determined to uproot the French presence on the Missouri River.

In the summer of 1720, Governor Don Antonio Valverde y Cosio of New Mexico dispatched Don Pedro Villasur to reconnoiter French strength in the Missouri valley. Villasur's expedition included at least 50 Spanish soldiers and 60 Pueblo Indian allies. Several Padouca scouts led the caravan from Santa Fe northeast toward the Missouri River. A priest serving as a chaplain accompanied the caravan with the holy sacraments of the Catholic Church. Pierre Boisbriant, the French commander at Kaskaskia, came to believe the entire Spanish expedition numbered over 250 people.

As the expedition neared the confluence of the Platte and Loup rivers in southeast Nebraska, Skidi Pawnee and Otoe scouts watched them. Already within the French sphere of influence, they attacked the Spanish caravan on or about August 14 with guns as well as the traditional lances and bow and arrows. The Padouca sensed danger and fled before the assault began. Twenty-five Spaniards, including Villasur, and eleven Pueblo Indians were killed in the battle. Alonso Rael de Aguiler recalled that twelve of the party fled with the bulk of the horse herd "having left in camp all their equipage and provisions." The warriors stopped to plunder the booty of the camp, buying the survivors' time to escape.

There are multiple contradictory accounts of the Villasur battle. Most authorities accept the one given above. A Spanish document reported that the "Pawnee and their allies" had defeated Villasur, and it appears the Missouria may have had a hand in the fight. A Missouria headman told Bourgmont in 1724: "We love the French people and naturally hate the Spaniards and Englishman. We proved it three winters ago. The Otoptata [Otoes] Panimaha [Skidi Pawnee] and ourselves completely defeated a large party of Spaniards who came to settle down among us."

Captain Testard de Montigny wrote in 1722 that the Spanish expedition from New Mexico had attacked two villages of the Otoe, intending to drive into the Illinois Country. Inhabitants of a third Otoe village, he said, finally ambushed and destroyed the Spaniards. Jean Bernard Bossu in 1756 said the Missouria had captured the Spanish priest and taken him to their village. "He had a very fine horse, and the Missourites took pleasure to see him ride it which he did very skillfully." One day, while giving a demonstration of his horsemanship he made good his escape. Le Page Du Pratz, the Dutch explorer, published a story in 1758 describing the expedition's plan to invade the Illinois Country by first destroying the Missouria:

> The Spaniards, as well as our other neighbors, being continually
> jealous of our superiority over them, formed a design of establish-

ing themselves among the Missouris, about forty leagues from the Illinois, in order to limit our boundaries westward. They judged it necessary, for the security of their colony, entirely to cut off the Missouris, and for that purpose they courted the friendship of the Osages, whose assistance they thought would be of service to them in their enterprise, and who were generally at enmity with the Missouris. A company of Spaniards, men, women, and soldiers, accordingly set out from Santa Fe, having a Dominican for their chaplain, and an engineer for their guide and commander. The caravan was furnished with horses and all other kinds of beasts necessary; for it is one of their prudent maxims, to send off all those things together. By a fatal mistake the Spaniards arrived first among the Missouris, whom they mistook for the Osages, and imprudently discovering their hostile intentions, they were themselves surprised and cut off by those whom they intended for destruction. The Missouris some time afterward dressed themselves with the ornaments of the chapel; and carried them in a kind of triumphant procession to the French commandant among the Illinois.

Boisbriant reported the arrival of sixty mounted Missouria warriors some bearing what appeared to be Lacrosse sticks. These were scalps stretched on a willow pole. The leader rode a horse with a Spanish saddle and silver bit. Father Benat, the post chaplain, was horrified, for around the neck of the horse was hung the Holy Communion chalice. The Missouria headman wore the chasuble (Mass vestment) and around his neck hung a paten used for serving communion bread during Holy Mass. Other Missouria warriors bore various pieces of Spanish accoutrements and church vessels. The leader indicated that the Black Robe in the Spanish party had been spared because he was dressed like a woman. No doubt he was thought to be *mihxoge,* a holy person. The Missouria wanted to exchange the Catholic religious ornaments for items they could use. An amused Boisbriant made the exchange and gave them gifts for their part in routing the Spanish. That night the people of Kaskaskia gathered at the Missouria campfire and watched the warriors dance a scalp dance.

LePage Du Pratz's version places the battle in central Missouri, which is incorrect, but he apparently saw physical evidence taken in the battle. "Along with the ornaments they brought a Spanish map, which seemed to me to be a better draft of the west part of our colony." Another account states it was the Pawnee whom the Spaniards intended to turn against the Otoe. The Spaniards knew the Otoe had close ties to the French but assumed the Pawnee did not since they had been trading buffalo robes for Spanish horses. The Otoe could speak Pawnee and would have understood the Spaniards' intended deception. If the Otoe did learn of it, the Spaniards were doomed because the Skidi Pawnee at this time had friendly relations with the Otoe and Missouria.

To justify their humiliating defeat at the hands of Indians, the Spanish claimed that French troops had been present at the battle. A painted buffalo hide from the period depicting the battle is in the Palace of the Governors in Santa Fe, New Mexico. It shows Indian warriors and French troops wearing tricornes. However, Boisbriant said no Frenchmen were present and that they only learned of the battle from the Indians themselves. With each French and Spanish retelling of the battle, errors and fabrications appear to have crept into the account, which explains the multiple versions. The possibility exists that the Missouria were not in the battle but later acquired Spanish artifacts from their Otoe kinsmen and then presented them to the French in order to ingratiate themselves and receive gifts.

Bourgmont and his son returned to Louisiana in September of 1722. Bourgmont was extremely ill on his arrival and did not recover sufficiently to travel to the Missouria villages until February of 1723. His expedition received fewer men and supplies than he had been promised. The Company of the Indies, which had exclusive trade and supply rights in Louisiana and Illinois, had gone bankrupt. John Law, the head of the company, was out of power, and the colonies of New France were in an economic shambles. Materials and foodstuffs were in short supply; many soldiers deserted for lack of pay while others were sick from fevers and malnutrition. Near Cahokia in present-day Illinois, Bourgmont's party received a reinforcement of six soldiers led by Ensign Louis Groston de St. Ange de Bellerive. Father Jean Paul Mercier, a missionary to the Tamaroa Indians, also joined the party.

Bourgmont's expedition received a boost from the Missouria themselves. They heard of his coming, and a party traveled over two hundred miles from their village to meet him in Cahokia. They welcomed him back with songs and dances and caresses. They were overjoyed to see his now nine-year-old son who had been called "Petit Missouri," or Little Missouri, by the French court. Without the assistance of the Missouria, Bourgmont's expedition would have collapsed.

In late fall Bourgmont reached the site where he would build Fort Orleans. The spot was on the north bank of the Missouri River in

In a map drawn by Jean Baptiste Bourginon d'Anville in 1732 and published in 1752, this detail from "Caret de Louisiane" shows the locations of
the Missouria and Little Osage villages in relation to Fort Orleans. The "R.
au Vermillion" is the Lamine and "Pierre a fleche" is the Arrow Rock bluff,
an important source of flint for the Oneota and their descendants, the Missouria. (Courtesy of the David Rumsey Map Collection)

present-day Carroll County, opposite the Missouria and Little Osage
villages. The fort was constructed over the winter of 1723–1724 and
named in honor of the Duke of Orleans, who was acting as regent for
six-year-old king Louis XV of France. A drawing published around
1727 shows extensive plans for the fort and associated structures, but
there is some doubt that they were ever completed as drawn. However the fort was a clear signal to Spain and the Indian nations that
France intended to stay on the Missouri.

Bourgmont hired Missouria women to cut the prairie grasses and
make thatch roofs for the fort's structures. The construction of the
fort may have encouraged the Missouria to completely abandon the
Utz site and move to Gumbo Point. Raids by the Sac and Fox had

increased, and the Missouria possibly believed the proximity of the fort and the Little Osage village would enhance their security.

Indian settlements were known for large numbers of *sukéñi*, dogs, which were close in appearance and behavior to their wolf ancestors. When the Lewis and Clark Expedition camped near the Gumbo Point in June 1804, Sergeant Patrick Gass wrote that they had reached the "village de pero." This was probably an inaccurate rendering of the Spanish "perro," and he meant "the village of dogs." There is some question since place-names in Louisiana retained their French pronunciation. It may have been a Spanish nickname for the Missouria village as Siouan towns were not named in the fashion of European villages.

Bourgmont had problems with the Indian dogs. While in the Missouria village, seven of fourteen sows that had been brought from the Illinois Country were lost in the woods or killed by dogs. He built an enclosure at the fort to protect his hogs and chickens from marauding dogs of the visiting Kansa. Village dogs, however, cleaned up food refuse in camps and warned of strangers approaching, and they were also a source of meat for a quick meal. Dog bones showing signs of butchering and cooking have been found on Oneota and Missouria archaeological sites. Boiled dog was a delicacy served to honored guests in some tribes.

Two of Bourgmont's officers, Lieutenants Lamase and Belisle, were jealous of Bourgmont's authority and relationship with the Missouria. They frequently wrote to his superiors accusing him of misconduct. They had been profiteering from the expedition, and Bourgmont reprimanded them for their conduct. Two Missouria headmen who could speak French overheard Pradel and Belisle complaining and reported to Bourgmont, "Chief Pradel is swearing against you and calling you names, crazy and a bad chief." Bourgmont rebuked the two officers and reminded them that he alone understood the temperament of the Missouria. Disunity and rebellion in the ranks created a dangerous situation, as the Missouria would perceive grumbling as a sign of weakness they could exploit. The Missouria could easily have avenged the insults by taking the heads of the two officers, but they did not. Bourgmont was married into the tribe, making him family, and family honor was a deadly serious matter among the Southern Siouan peoples.

French colonial officials soon found themselves in a quandary. Part of Bourgmont's mission was to make peace with the Padouca.

This alliance could help France realize its goal of reaching the Spanish mines of New Mexico and the Pacific, but it would also eliminate the highly profitable French trade in Padouca captives. Indians took captives in war, which Europeans generally mischaracterized as "slaves." The captives did not work to support the lifestyle of an owner, as in the European and American concept of slavery. Warriors were rarely taken alive, and if captured, they did not expect to survive long. Many of the captives were young people, children, and women taken either to replace relatives who had died in warfare or from disease or accidents or simply to introduce "new blood" into the tribe. Adoption was a serious, spiritual matter among Indians and the process was accompanied by much ceremony. Indian captives seem to have accepted the idea that once adopted, their identity changed and they were "reborn" as part of a new family. A famous example of this concept was Sacagawea, the Shoshone woman who accompanied the Lewis and Clark Expedition. She was captured as a young girl by the Hidatsa and adopted into their tribe. When the expedition met the Shoshone, the chief of the advance party was Sacagawea's own brother. Had she desired to return to the Shoshone she could have told her brother, and no one could have prevented her return.

The arrival of the French soon altered the concept of captives among the Indian nations. The French needed laborers to work their farms and plantations in lower Louisiana and the West Indies. The closest non-European population for a source of "slaves" was Indians. By 1700, Frenchmen were trading brandy and merchandise to the Missouria, Osage, Kansa, and Illini for captives taken in war. The Jesuits decried this situation and complained that the traders were constantly inciting the Indians to make war in order to buy their captives and then sell them as slaves.

Officially, France outlawed the practice of Indian slavery in Louisiana and the Illinois Country. However, the lawless *"courier de bois,"* woods runners, acted as field agents in securing slaves. One official report noted that plantation owners "get as many savage slaves as they wish on the River of the Missouris, whom they use to cultivate their farms." The surplus, the report noted, "was sold to the English of Carolina" a grievous breach of the law since England was the enemy of France. However laws and decrees of the king were largely unenforceable in New France. With the colony in an economic depression, local officials wanted to make money any way they could.

Stopping the slave trade could also alienate or anger the Missouria and Osage, who were already important French allies.

Bienville wrote to Boisbriant in Illinois "however easy M. de Bourgmont may believe it is possible to make peace with the Padoucas, we should drop the idea and push our tribes [Missouria and Osage] toward war with them to trade in slaves for the account of the Company." Bienville wanted the promised supplies withheld from the Bourgmont peace mission. He directed Boisbriant to push Bourgmont to incite the Missouria and Osage to make war on the troublesome Fox. However Bienville's letter did not reach Illinois until January 1724, after Bourgmont was already at the Missouria village.

Bourgmont was quick to reply to Bienville's sabotage of his mission. "For me, with the Indians nothing is impossible. I make them do what they have never done." He pointed out that when the Otoe and Kansa had robbed French traders, he made them pay back double. He broke up an attempt by the Otoe and Ioway to ally themselves with the Fox and Dakota against France. A Missouria warrior killed a Frenchman, and Bourgmont had the man killed in the middle of the village by having his own brother shoot him with arrows. He wrote, "To show me there were no hard feelings, the brother sent me a nice present on my arrival here three and half months ago." Finally he pointed out that the king of France had already paid for the expense of making peace with the Padouca. Boisbriant relented and sent the supplies along with a mining engineer, Phillipe de La Renaudier, to Fort Orleans.

Bourgmont dispatched Ensign St. Ange with a boatload of supplies to the Kansa Nation on June 25, 1724. On July 3, he departed Fort Orleans with an escort of 100 Missouria and 64 Osages, following a well-used trail on the north side of the Missouri River. On the night of July 7, they camped on the Missouri River opposite the Kansa village near present-day Leavenworth, Kansas. The following morning the Frenchmen crossed the river in a pirogue and swam their horses over. The Indians crossed on rafts that, Du Pratz wrote, the Missouria wove from the cane growing on the riverbank. In 1804 Lewis and Clark, referring to Du Pratz's report, noted the absence of cane on the Missouri River in their time.

The Kansa greeted Bourgmont in peace with sacred pipes and a present of two horses. Seven headmen spoke in turn, saying they were "true chiefs," and expressed their respect and admiration for Bourgmont, saying they wished to accompany him on his mission to the Padouca. When the speeches were finished, the sacred pipe was passed and smoked to confirm their words. Bourgmont was carried on a bison robe to the lodge of the lead headman, where there were more speeches and presents of peltries and food given to the Frenchmen. This type of reception would be given to an honored person visiting a Missouria or Osage village as well.

St. Ange had not yet arrived with the boat, and a Frenchman and a Missouria reported the supplies were safe but the boat was stalled, as several men were stricken with fever. Five Frenchmen and nine Missourias were dispatched to help get the supplies to the village. Bourgmont sent four Missouria runners about 150 miles to the north to invite the Otoes to the proceedings. They returned the next evening with news that the Otoe were on their way. Fevers spread throughout the Kansa village. On July 11, one of two Padouca captives whom Bourgmont planned to return as a sign of his goodwill died. Bourgmont himself was struck by fever. On July 16, St. Ange finally arrived with the boat. With his supplies and trade goods in hand, Bourgmont began negotiating with the Kansa for horses to make the journey to the Padouca. The haggling did not go well, and the Kansa scowled and sulked. One warrior rode off in disgust, a serious breach of etiquette. Bourgmont became angry and ordered all trading suspended and went off to walk alone along the river.

Seeing his anger was genuine, the tribal elders held a council. Afterward a dozen headmen approached Bourgmont and begged forgiveness for their conduct. They wept at his feet and caressed him saying, "We promise never to abandon you" and pledged to send five hundred warriors along on the peace expedition. They also gave him a present of five captives, two horses, and several bundles of peltries. Bourgmont accepted the gifts, but he told the Kansa if they did not complete the peace mission he would make them regret it.

At this point a new problem arose that threatened to derail the mission. The lead headman of the Kansa wanted to give his fourteen-year-old daughter in marriage to Bourgmont. This would create family ties and obligate Bourgmont to protect and favor the Kansa. He replied that the French could not have two wives and he already had a Missouria wife. Actually, he also had a French wife and a child born during his last visit to France. The Kansa did not accept that explanation since in Siouan cultures a man having more than one wife was commonplace. Bourgmont then pointed out that his son "Petit Missouri" was only ten years old but that he would consent to his son's marriage to the chief's daughter in ten more years if he wanted her. The Kansa agreed to keep the chief's daughter for Petit Missouri until he was old enough.

Bourgmont began preparing the expedition into Padouca country, but the fevers reached epidemic proportion. The Osage became frightened and fled the Kansa village to avoid the disease. Bourgmont's able-bodied men had to build rafts and transport the sick back to the Missouria village. Of the 164 Indians who had accompanied Bourgmont, only 20 remained. The headman, probably Bourgmont's father-in-law, told him "he would stay with him to the death."

On the morning of July 24 the expedition got under way. La Renaudiere counted "300 Indian warriors, two head chiefs, 14 war chiefs, 300 women, 500 children and 300 dogs dragging freight on travois." He saw dogs dragging loads of 300 pounds and saw girls as young as 12 carry 100 pounds for two or three leagues. The column slowly plodded across the plains toward the southwest.

By July 31 Bourgmont had become so ill that he could not stay on a horse, and he had to be carried back to the Kansa village on a litter. La Renaudiere completed the mission, and the Kansa and Padouca smoked the sacred pipe and made peace. The Padouca were now officially allies of France, but the alliance never achieved the lasting results for which Bourgmont had hoped. Following the peace mission, he was directed to bring several Indian "chiefs" to France. He held a council with the Missouria, Osage, and Otoe on November 19, 1724, to discuss the journey. An unnamed Missouria headman spoke:

> Our father, when you came to our lands on your return from across the Great Lake [Atlantic Ocean] you spoke to us on behalf of the great Onontio [an Algonquin Indian term for the Governor of New France, Philippe de Rigaud Vaudreuil] who is the absolute master of your people and who illuminates the entire world, like the sun. You have told us that he has asked you to bring with you several chiefs of our nation when you return to his land. You see us now all assembled here to consider this matter. Although we may be unrefined, we judge, nevertheless, that it would be shameful for our tribe not to obey the request made by the great chief, whom we have heard of since we were born. Here are four chiefs, whom we place in your charge, and the daughter of the head chief of our tribe, so that you may conduct them to the country, which is the source of our fusils [guns], gunpowder, and generally all the merchandise we have.

The headman reaffirmed the intention of the Missouria to keep the peace recently made with the Padouca and expressed a fear of "our enemies the Foxes" if the French should abandon them. He reminded Bourgmont how they assisted the Skidi Pawnee and Otoe in destroying the Villasur expedition. The headman expressed confidence in the words of Bourgmont and prayed for Wakanda to have pity on him, and promised to weep for those departing. The headman concluded by saying, "We hope that our people will not return naked or empty-handed since they are going to that country where all that we prize is made." The headman's speech was printed in the newspaper *Mercure de France* but had probably undergone extensive editing by the time it was published. Although the core sentiments may be correct, the phraseology is characteristically French rather than Siouan.

Bourgmont, his Missouria wife, and three headmen each from the Missouria, Osage, and Otoe nations departed Fort Orleans in November of 1724. They picked up five Illini headmen and a Jesuit priest at Fort de Chartres. They reached New Orleans on January 9, 1725, but to save expenses, the Company of the Indies would allow only one headman of each tribe to go on the trip. Their ship, the *Bellone,* sank near Dauphine Island on April 2, destroying the possessions of the Indians and many of Bourgmont's and Governor Bienville's private documents and correspondence. Undoubtedly, these lost documents would have yielded more information about the Missouria during this early period.

The group finally made the Atlantic crossing aboard a ship named the *La Gironde.* Scurvy and malaria afflicted the passengers, and one Indian died on the voyage, though his tribe was not specified. The party finally arrived in Paris, France, on September 20, 1725. Articles in the *Mercure de France* gushed over the Indians, their appearance, their speeches, and the gifts lavished on them. The *Mercure* reported; "Their astonishment at the beauty of things they had seen was inexpressible . . . they wanted to know how the birds and animals spouted water through their mouths," a reference to the many fountains in Paris. The Indians were given lavish parties, met King Louis XV, and hunted deer in his private preserve. They attended the opera and performed their native dances at the Theatre des Comediens Italiens to the great delight of French audiences.

Bourgmont's Missouria wife became a special favorite of the French courtesans. The *Mercure* identified her as "Ignon Ouaconisen" but also called her the "Savagesse." She was given a flame-colored linen dress with a design of gold flowers, a petticoat of the same fabric, a hoop petticoat, two corsets, six blouses, six pairs of puffed sleeves and gold and silver ribbons and silk stockings. Apparently she would not wear hats and went around bareheaded. The "Missouri Princess" has become the subject of romantic speculation throughout history although most details of her life are unknown.

The Indians met formally with the directors of the Company of the Indies on November 8. The Missouria headman said,

> Twelve moons have passed since we left our homes to come here. One of our chiefs died on the way; others had to be left behind on the coast. We have been told that the King and the Company requested the presence of representatives of each of our tribes. Here we are before you, without knowing what you wish of us.

The question went unanswered. The Indians were just given more gifts and told to always obey the king of France and his agents. They were given parting gifts by King Louis on November 28, gold medals and chains, fusils, swords, watches, and a painting showing the royal audience with the Indians. The company gave the Indians a large number of presents. The Indians were embarrassed and ashamed, as they could give nothing in return, having lost their gifts and personal possessions in the sinking of the *Bellone*.

Ignon Ouaconisen was baptized at the Cathedral of Notre Dame, where she married Sergeant Dubois of Bourgmont's command. Bourgmont's life was taking a new direction. The marriage relieved him of any responsibility for her. The Catholic Church did not recognize Missouria custom so her prior marriage to Bourgmont was not a problem to the Church. Sergeant Dubois and his new wife returned to Louisiana along with the Indian leaders. A mural in the Missouri state capitol building depicts the "Missouri Princess" and her new husband being received by the Missouria tribe.

Bourgmont stayed in France and was elevated to the rank of squire. His coat of arms was "a naked savage, reclining on a mountain of silver" against an azure background. He returned to his French wife Jacqueline Bouvet des Bordeaux and acquired a large estate. He never returned to Louisiana and died in 1734. His son, Petit Missouri, dropped completely from historical accounts. There is no mention of him following Bourgmont's expedition to the Kansa village. Perhaps he lived the remainder of his life among his Missouria relatives.

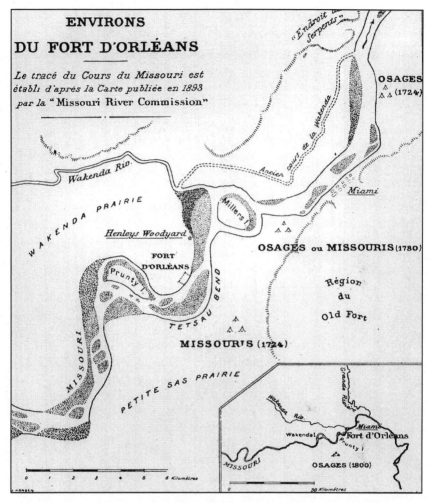

Baron Marc de Villiers was the first person to extensively study documents related to Fort Orleans. He developed this map of "Environs du Fort Orleans" in 1925 in an attempt to locate the site of the fort and neighboring Indian villages. (Courtesy of the State Historical Society Missouri)

Du Pratz reported a horrific end to Fort Orleans; "After the departure of that commandant, they [Missouria] murdered all the garrison, not a single Frenchman having escaped to carry the news: nor could it be ever known whether it happened through the fault of the French, or through treachery." Dumont du Montigny went so far as to say that Sergeant Dubois was killed in this massacre and that Ignon

Ouaconisen renounced her Christianity and reverted to a "savage state." No mention of a massacre exists in any known official French document. The head of the Company of the Indies signed an order to "abandon the Missouri post" in October of 1727, declaring it was not worth the expense of maintaining it for the company. A letter dated April 1, 1729, written by Governor M. M. Perrier in New Orleans said that Fort Orleans "had been relieved." Without Bourgmont's drive and oversight, the fort had simply languished.

The Missouria were fairly reliable allies of the French and needed their guns and ammunition in their ongoing fight against the Fox and their Sac allies. Massacring the garrison would not have been in their best interest. Evidence suggests that the Fox ambushed Sergeant Dubois and his detachment on the lower Missouri River as they traveled to Illinois. This may have been the source of the fort massacre story. Ignon Ouaconisen married another Frenchman named Marin and had two children with him. She had by then taken a first name, "François." Jean Bernard Bossu met her while living in Kaskaskia in 1752 and thought she had never returned to the Missouria village.

While at Fort Orleans, Father Mercier had written to his superiors that the Osages had asked for missionaries. After the post was abandoned, he gave up his missionary activity, stating that the Missouria were "too dangerous" without the presence of troops. Tribal beliefs and ceremonies were rooted in centuries of tradition and would not be lightly discarded. Father Mercier's experience indicates the Missouria tolerated the presence of the Black Robes only when necessary to enhance trade relations. Fort Orleans may have been briefly reestablished. French documents dating between 1736 and 1742 discuss traders going to "the Post of the Missouris" to trade with the Indians residing there and the neighboring area. However, it is not clear if this was indeed Fort Orleans or another post built near the Missouria villages.

New France was divided into districts as regional trade networks developed with the native peoples. French Canadians became jealous when John Law's Company of the West, then later the Company of the Indies, managed to have the Illinois Country placed under the administration of the Louisiana Territory. Lucrative fur-trading markets with the various bands of Dakota Sioux in Minnesota and Iowa were disrupted. Some French Canadians began using Indian tribes as mercenaries to destroy their competitors in Illinois. *Courier de bois* told the Fox that the Illinois Creole French were "other white men" outside the protection of Onontio, the governor general. The Fox,

Courier de bois, French-Canadian woodsmen, rapidly spread westward from the Great Lakes to the Mississippi and Missouri River, bringing guns, metal, tools, cloth, beads and liquor to the Missouria. (Courtesy of the State Historical Society of Missouri)

again in alliance with the Mascouten and Kickapoo, began attacking the Illini Indians and trade routes in the Illinois Country. In June of 1723, the Cahokias fought with the Fox near their village. A group of Missouria returning from Fort Chartres found a dead Fox warrior near the mouth of the Meramec River and sent the head to their Cahokia allies. Attacks in 1724 and 1725 caused the fur trade in the Illinois Country to collapse. In 1726 the Illinois French reached out to the Missouria, Osage, and Otoes for help. This threat on their western flank blocked the Fox from trading with the Dakota Sioux. Despite the military assistance the Missouria had provided since 1712, some French officials found them bothersome and a nuisance. Commander Boisbriant at Fort Chartres cynically noted that the "Missouria were constantly in turmoil and sought only presents" when they came to the post. However, France wanted to annihilate the Fox, and they needed the help of the Missouria to do that. Sensing defeat, the Kickapoo switched allegiance, and in August of 1730, France's Indian allies besieged the Fox at Starved Rock, Illinois. St. Ange arrived on the scene with 100 French militia and 400 Missouria and Illini warriors. The fighting reduced the Fox population from about 3,000 to 1,000. As the French closed in for the final blow, the Kickapoo scouts took pity on their former allies and led the French army on a wild goose chase, buying time for the Fox survivors to flee to the Des Moines River, where they took refuge with the Sac tribe. This led to the amalgamation of the two tribes as the Sac and Fox Nation.

Indian trouble was brewing elsewhere in New France. The Chickasaw Nation traded with the British and, at their invitation, moved their villages to sites directly on the Mississippi River near present-day Memphis, Tennessee. Their presence cut the line of communication and supply between the capital of New Orleans and the Illinois Country. Chickasaw war parties raided French outposts as far north as the Ohio and Wabash rivers. To make matters worse, fighting with the Fox flared up again in 1732.

In 1734 the Big Osage killed a slave and an *engagé* from Arkansas Post. Fearing a cut-off of trade, the Osages persuaded the Missouria to serve as liaisons and deliver a message to Bienville, now the commandant at Fort Chartres. The Missouria reported that the Osage apologized for the murders and promised to mend their ways. Facing trouble with the Fox in the north and Chickasaw in the south, Bienville wrote, "I do not believe that it suits the state of our affairs to push this matter any farther. We do not need to see new wars." The stage was now set: the Missouria and Osage could kill Frenchmen if they saw a reason for it and then simply ask for forgiveness from government officials. In 1734 and 1735 they killed at least eleven French traders. The government was more concerned about maintaining the alliances than they were with the deaths of a few unlicensed traders.

In October of 1735, the French armed a joint expedition of 400 Missouria and Kansa warriors to attack the fortified Sac and Fox village on the Des Moines River. At the approach of the French-led Indians, the Sac and Fox abandoned the village and scattered on the prairie. The Missouria broke off the pursuit, leading the French to complain that nothing was achieved in the campaign. At the same time Captain Pierre D'Artguette at Kaskaskia was assembling an army to strike the Chickasaw, but he had to postpone the attack because the Missouria were still engaged against the Sac and Fox in the north. D'Artguette assembled another army at Kaskaskia in February 1736. Over 200 Illini and Missouria warriors "properly bedecked in paint and feathers, in their log canoes" joined 30 regular soldiers and 100 militiamen. Soon Cahokia, Mitchigamea, Ottawa, Miami, and Piankeshaw warriors and militia from other parts of New France arrived. Bienville was to march north from New Orleans with yet another force of militia and Indian allies, thus striking the Chickasaw with a two-pronged attack.

The campaign went badly for the French. The Chickasaw villages were heavily fortified and well supplied with British guns. The separate French forces were unable to coordinate their attacks. Captain D'Artguette was severely wounded, and he and fifteen other Frenchmen were captured and burned to death by the Chickasaw. The French accused the Miami of betrayal and the Missouria and Illini of "running like sheep." This was not the first or last time European leaders blamed their failed military campaigns on improperly used Indian auxiliaries. Fighting in thick forests, besieging fortified towns, and launching massed frontal attacks were concepts of warfare alien to the Missouria and their allies who were primarily horse raiders and light cavalry of the prairies.

The Chickasaw resumed their harassment of the French in the fall of 1739. The French amassed a new army of "200 Negroes, 200 Canadians, 100 Illinois militia, 400 soldiers from the colony, 50 free Negroes, and 300 marines." Another 600 Indian warriors from bands of Shawnee, Abnaki, Iroquois, Chitimacha, Choctaw, and Cherokee joined the force. Once again a large contingent of Missouria warriors arrived to aid the French. An officer named Fontaine Meine reported that by November the Indians wanted to go home and could be persuaded to remain "only by giving them wine." Quarrels broke out whenever the French Canadians and the Indians got drunk. The Chickasaw sued for peace in April of 1740. The army broke up, and the Missouria went home.

In July of 1740, an Illini Indian reported at Fort Chartres that the Osage had killed several Frenchmen in the Arkansas District and one in the Missouri District. The Missouria killed a Frenchman named La Grillade and openly talked of murdering yet others. To counter these ominous developments, Joseph Deruisseau received an exclusive concession for the fur trade of the Missouri River. He explained to Governor Bienville that the Missouria had complaints against the French-Canadian *voyageurs* for cheating them and treating them violently. There had also been reports of the French Canadians seducing, then abducting, Missouria women from their villages. The *voyageurs* and *courier de bois* supplied brandy to the Indians, which fomented violence that resulted in murders among both Indians and whites. A trader named Joseph Adam transported three hundred bottles of brandy to trade with the Missouria and Little Osage. A large number of glass bottle fragments found at Gumbo Point may have been part of his cargo. These unlicensed traders had no concern for the law or France's relations with the Indian nations. Their only concern was personal profit, and they were a threat to France's hold on the Missouri Valley.

Deruisseau built his small post near present-day Fort Leavenworth, Kansas, and named it Fort Cavignal. His goal was not only to trade for peltries from the Missouria, Osage, Kansa, Otoe, and Pawnee, but also to block the unlicensed traders from traveling on the Missouri River. But this was an impossible task for just one small post. The Indians were content to do business with the unlicensed traders and not report them to officials. If the traders cheated or crossed them, it was a simple matter to deal with them. More unlicensed traders and hunters were probably killed in the remote vastness of the Louisiana Territory than are known to history.

In 1749, the British attempted to incite the Illini, Miami, and Piankeshaw to rise up against the French. The British reached out to the Missouria and the Big and Little Osages to join the rebellion, the reward being cheaper but higher quality English merchandise. The Missouria and the Little Osage chose to remain loyal to the French, possibly because their bitter enemies, the Sac and Fox, were now steady clients of the British. An example of the continuing animosity between the Missouria and the Sac and Fox occurred in September of 1741; British-armed Sac and Fox warriors attacked a large party of Illini coming down the Mississippi in canoes and killed several. The French reported that when the Illini identified themselves, a Sac leader replied, "My brothers we are sorry for what has happened . . . we believed you were Missouris." The French correctly feared the incident would lead to open warfare between the Sac and Fox and the Illini.

In return for the presents they received from the English traders, the Big Osage attacked the Caddoes and the Quapaw, both allies of the French. However, these attacks did not help the British position. British supplies simply allowed the Big Osage to act on territorial impulses and longstanding tribal animosities. The Big Osage were expanding to the west away from the scene of English and French confrontation.

The loyalty of the Missouria and Little Osage to the French continued to be put to the test. In the fall of 1751, English colliers or wampum belts (necklaces of war beads) and presents were reported to be circulating among the Missouria and Osage. At Fort Chartres, Major Richard McCarty, an Irishman turned French subject, assured Governor Pierre de Rigard de Vaudriel on April 28, 1752, that the Missouria, Cahokia, Peoria, Big and Little Osage were all solid allies of the French. British attempts to trade with these Indians added to tensions between the two European powers. The British used the Illini to woo their old friends the Missouria and Osage. Governor Kerelec of Louisiana reported in 1754 that the Missouria and Little Osage were still very much attached to the French. However, the French were forced to constantly assess their relationship with these tribes. The bewildering situation was the result of the Missouria and Little Osage playing both sides against each other to gain presents and trade concessions.

The tensions between France and England finally erupted into open war in the summer of 1754. The Seven Years War in Europe was the French and Indian War in North America. France recruited its Indian allies to fight against British forces. Major McCarty recruited the Missouria, Osage, and Kansa at Fort Chartres. About 200 warriors made the march from the fort over 800 miles to the Monongahela River in western Pennsylvania. On July 9 1755, near Fort Duquesne, French and Indian forces decimated the expeditionary force of General Edward Braddock. Despite early victories, the French could not overcome British naval blockades of North America. Outposts were closed and trade supplies for the Indians became especially scarce.

Many tribes lost the incentive to the fight against the British and, worse, the smallpox broke out and spread among Indians throughout the western territories.

With the Treaty of Paris signed in February 1763, the war between England and France came to an end. France surrendered its claim to territory east of the Mississippi River and Canada to the British. It later transferred the Louisiana Territory to Spain to keep it out of English hands. However, Great Britain remained interested in this territory because of its rich fur resources. Spain was a comparatively weak nation and slow to establish its claims on Louisiana, so many French officials continued in office. Britain was unable to take advantage of this situation due to resistance of Indians in the Great Lakes region led by Pontiac, the great Ottawa chief. The Indians wanted the French to remain their "fathers" and trading partners and fought the British for the next two years.

4

Turmoil in Upper Louisiana

Unaware of the changes in government resulting from the Treaty of Paris, Pierre Liguest Laclede left Fort Chartres in the Illinois Country in the winter of 1763 to construct a new trading post on the Mississippi River. He took along his stepson, Auguste Chouteau, then about fourteen years old. After selecting a location near the mouth of the Missouri, he left Chouteau in charge of laying out the plan of the new town while he returned to Fort Chartres for supplies. In June of 1764, Louis St. Ange de Bellerive took command of Fort Chartres and prepared to turn it over to the British. St. Ange wrote, "The Missouri Indians arrived at Illinois on July 17 for fear of another attack by the Great Osage Indians. I am attempting to conclude a peace agreement between these two Indian groups; and I have succeeded in persuading the Missouri Indians to return to their land in order to avoid great expense to the King." He did not specify what prompted the Big Osage to threaten the Missouria.

Laclede encouraged the French families in Illinois to join his new settlement. In the meantime, nearly the entire Missouria tribe, some six hundred persons, arrived at Laclede's settlement. Their intent to settle there permanently became obvious. The inhabitants of St. Louis were nervous about having a large body of Indians permanently encamped near them. Chouteau described how his stepfather handled the Missouria:

Monsieur de Laclede arrived and immediately the chief of the Missouris came to see him, in order to hold a council. The result of the council was that they were worthy of pity; that they were like the ducks and the bustards [wading birds] who sought open water in order to rest and procure an easy subsistence; that they did not find any place more suitable, in their opinion than the place they were. Upon that they said many things, which always amounted to this–they desired to settle where they were.

Laclede waited a day to give the Missouria his reply. He didn't want them there. He knew that if the Sac and Fox, Ottawa, Potawatomie, or Kickapoo attacked the Missouria, St. Louis residents would be caught in the cross fire. Also, the Missouria had admitted to Laclede that they could "procure an easy subsistence." They were constantly seeking gifts and food and could consume all the foodstuffs and supplies of the settlement. Laclede exercised his considerable diplomacy in dealings with the Indians. He called another council and firmly addressed the Missouria:

You told me yesterday that you were like the ducks and bustards, who traveled until they found a fine country, where there was beautiful open water, that they might rest there and obtain an easy living, and that you, the Missouris, who were worthy of pity, resembled them, because you traveled like them to find a place to settle yourselves, and that you did not find one more suitable than where you are at present; that you wished to form a village around my house, where we should live in the greatest friendship. I will reply to you in a few words, and I will say to you that if you followed the example of the ducks and the bustards in settling yourselves then you followed bad guides, who have no foresight because if they had any they would not put themselves in open water so that the eagles and birds of prey could discover them easily, which would never happen if they were in a woody place and covered with brush. You Missouria, you will not be eaten by eagles; but these men who have waged war against you for a long time past, who are in great numbers against you who are few, will kill your warriors, because they will offer resistance, and will make your women and children slaves.

Laclede warned the Missouria that six or seven hundred warriors under Pontiac were waiting near Fort Chartres to make war on the English. If they learned of the presence of the Missouria at St. Louis, he had no doubt they would quickly come across the Mississippi to

Pierre Laclede Ligueist founded St. Louis in 1764. His knowledge of Indian customs and diplomacy was extremely useful when the entire Missouria nation tried to settle at the fledgling settlement, threatening to overwhelm its resources. (Courtesy of the Missouri History Museum)

destroy them. In the most graphic terms, he described how the Missouria women and children would be torn to pieces and thrown to the dogs and birds of prey. Laclede finished his speech by saying, "Recollect, I speak as a good father; reflect well upon what I have just told you, and give me your answer this evening, I can not give you any longer time for I must return to Fort Chartres."

The whole nation came to Laclede and told him that "they had opened their ears wide to his discourse, and that they would follow

Laclede's trading headquarters in St. Louis were later used by the Spanish as the government house. Still later Auguste Chouteau added a second story and lived there. The foundations of this house was dug by Missouria women and children while the tribe was settled nearby. (Courtesy of the Missouri History Museum)

his advice." The Missouria asked Laclede to have pity on the women and children and give them provisions, powder, and lead so that they could hunt and defend themselves on the journey up the Missouri River. Laclede agreed but had to send to Cahokia for corn because there was not enough in St. Louis to feed them. After having been in St. Louis for at least fifteen days, the Missouria were provisioned with corn, gunpowder, lead, knives, and cloth, and they departed for their "ancient village" on the Missouri River.

During their stay, young Chouteau had paid the Missouria women and children for their work with vermilion, a red pigment used for body paint; verdigris, a green powder produced by oxidized copper; and sewing awls to dig the cellar of the trading house. "They dug the largest part of it, and carried the earth in wooden platters and baskets, which they bore upon their heads." The scene must have been reminiscent of how the Mississippians moved dirt when building mounds. Thus, in some respects, Missouria women and children literally helped lay the foundations of St. Louis.

Missouria, Osage, and Illini warriors gathered at Fort Chartres on April 4, 1765, and listened to St. Ange and Lieutenant Ross of the British army discuss the transfer of French Illinois to Great Britain. The Indians told the English officer, "Go away, go away and tell your chief that all red men want the English out of here." On October 10, 1765, the French *Fleur des Lis* was lowered at Fort Chartres, and the British Union Jack was raised in its place. Pontiac fought a hopeless, last-ditch campaign for France and the French fur trade, but his warriors were crushed, and the Indians finally accepted that the French were gone and the English were there to stay.

The French had transferred their holdings west of the Mississippi River to Spain in 1764. Spain was content to allow the French Creole population to retain control of the Louisiana territorial government. French laws were still in place as late as 1770. The upper half of Louisiana Territory was first called "Spanish Illinois" to distinguish it from "British Illinois" across the Mississippi River, and eventually it became "Upper Louisiana."

Just as they had done during the French regime, the British attempted to subvert the tribes on the Missouri River. British traders operated freely on the upper Mississippi and from there visited tribes along the Missouri River. In terms of quality and price, English merchandise was superior to that of the French and Spanish, and British traders worked hard to turn the Missouria and Osage against the Spanish.

In 1767, the British Union Jack was seen flying above the lodges of the Missouria and the Little Osage. St. Ange, now acting governor of Louisiana, sent the two tribes a message saying that the Spaniards would soon arrive and treat them as the French had. His appeal did not persuade the Missouria to break off relations with the British. This led Captain Pedro Gerardo de Vilemont to urge the building of a military post on the Missouri River. Governor Antonio de Ulloa followed up on the recommendation and ordered construction of two forts at the mouth of the Missouri River to prevent the entry of British traders. Fort San Carlos was located on the bluffs of the south bank overlooking the Missouri. A smaller blockhouse was placed in the river bottoms of the north bank. Captain Francisco Riú manned both installations with a total of just fourteen soldiers. To save on expenses, Riú was directed to feed the garrison from the "abundant wild cattle" (bison) found there.

Some may have difficulty understanding how the British were able to operate freely inside first French- and then Spanish-occupied territory. Most Europeans in the trans-Mississippi West were of French-Canadian or French Creole descent and were fluent in one or more native languages. These men were hardy *voyageurs* and *courier de bois* who knew the forests and prairies well. Most of the "British" traders coming out of the Illinois Country or Canada were not English but actually French Canadians who could blend in with the local populations. Traveling at night in canoes loaded with merchandise, they often slipped undetected past the forts on the river.

The origin of traders mattered little to the Missouria or the Osage. Like consumers today, they were looking for the best deals on goods that made life better or gave them an advantage over their neighbors. The Indians well understood the economic benefit they could gain when European powers competed for their trade. The Missouria and Little Osage successfully played British and Spanish interests against each other. Their villages on the Missouri River put them in a position to access or control traders from either empire going upriver.

Generous gift giving was a widespread practice among Indian nations, and the Missouria were no exception. Visiting dignitaries were given feasts and gifts such as horses, clothing, or blankets that the tribe may have had available, as the Kansa did when Bourgmont visited them. To openly admire an object in an Indian village was to receive it as a gift. Indians expected the same kind of generosity and hospitality in return when visiting St. Louis or Sainte Genevieve. The French understood this Indian practice and tried to follow it within reason. The Spanish government found the Indian practice tedious, irritating, and costly to their treasury. They tried to limit the amount of time that tribes could visit their settlements.

The possibility of generosity toward the Missouri River tribes depended on the money supplied to St. Louis from the central government in New Orleans. The subsidy for Upper Louisiana tended to fall short and arrive irregularly, leading the Indians to view the Spanish as miserly and stingy. Some officials were indeed miserly. Governor Antonio de Ulloa in 1768 banned traders from visiting Indian villages as a "cost saving measure." Missouria, Osage, Kansa, and Otoe people began arriving in St. Louis expressing anger over the governor's action. When Captain Francisco Riú held councils with the Indians, they walked out on him. The Missouria and Little Osage hinted that the Spanish settlements would suffer reprisals. They knew the British were quite willing to fill in the trade gap left by the Spanish.

The Osages began going to Kaskaskia, and Lieutenant Colonel John Wilkins reported that they complained "of their masters the French and Spaniards who are much displeased at their coming to trade with us." On May 5, 1769, the headmen of the Missouria and 42 warriors "brought great plenty to trade and talked much of their regard to the English." Wilkins gave them 6 gallons of rum and provisions. On May 8, as they prepared to depart, Wilkins offered them an unspecified present worth 20 pounds sterling, but they refused saying it was "insufficient." Wilkins reported the Missouria had been troublesome to him as well as to Commandant St. Ange in Spanish territory, "who treated them as they deserved."

On June 27, another large party of Missouria appeared at Kaskaskia. Wilkins gave them three gallons of rum, 6 pounds of gunpowder and 12 pounds of lead, a blanket, and further provisions. This party of Missouria also refused Wilkins's parting gift worth 20 pounds sterling. The Missouria and other tribes were very discriminating in what merchandise they accepted. Wilkins's gift was probably shoddy or cast-off merchandise, and the Indians took offense at his offer.

To counter trading with the British, Captain Francisco Riú finally ordered merchandise to be dispersed to the Missouria and Osage, and he informed Governor Ulloa that his endeavors had prevented a war. Ulloa tried to remain cordial to the British even as they kept reaching out to the Missouria and Little Osage. Indians from British Illinois began coming to St. Louis and asking for presents. This added to the strain the Spanish already faced in placating the Indian nations within their own territory. Yet they were hesitant to turn these "British" Indians away. Treating them well could thwart British activities in the region. Luis de Unzaga assumed control of Upper Louisiana in 1770 and noted, "The English had been courting the Little Osage and Missouries for several years with excessive presents." Emboldened by the steady supply of English trade goods and the weak policies of Spain, the Missouria and Little Osage began extorting traders on the Missouri River. Both tribes also began stealing horses in St. Louis and Sainte Genevieve.

Spanish relations with the Missouria and Little Osage continued to deteriorate. In the summer of 1772, the Missouria and Little Osage killed three hunters and captured two others on the Des Moines River. The Spanish were eventually able to secure the release of the two captives with gifts to the tribes. Lieutenant Governor Pedro Piernas railed against the two tribes for their raids on St. Louis and Sainte Genevieve and for their treatment of traders. However Piernas could do little to stop the problem.

Missouri's first European settlement, Ste. Genevieve, was established sometime between 1722 and 1749. Ste. Genevieve was also the scene of horse-stealing raids by the Missouria and their Little Osage allies during the Spanish regime. (Courtesy of the State Historical Society of Missouri)

Further emboldened by the impotent response, Missouria and Little Osage warriors broke into Fort San Carlos near St. Louis in July of 1772. They knocked down the five soldiers on duty and stripped the post of all its ammunition and provisions. The warriors entered St. Louis and began terrorizing the inhabitants. As a last act of defiance, the warriors raised a British flag in the middle of town. The citizens had enough and called the warriors' bluff. They restrained and reprimanded the Indians while they tore down the British flag.

This incident may have been part of what the Osages called a "bluff war." The Osage did not dispense death wantonly as Europeans were prone to believe. Death brought disharmony and imbalance in the universe. Because of that a "war movement" required the sanction of the elders and much ceremonial preparation. Killing without that sanction and preparation had no honor. The objective of "bluff war" was to achieve the goals of war by intimidating enemies rather than killing them if possible. Whether the Missouria shared the Osage concept of bluff war is unknown. However, had these warriors been part of a "war movement," the soldiers and citizens in St. Louis would have been killed outright.

Ironically, Spanish officials chose not to punish the Indians, probably fearing retaliation would lead to a real war. A large party of Potawatomie and Salteaux Ojibwa from British Illinois appeared in

St. Louis while the Little Osages were still camped nearby. In the ensuing fight, two Little Osage headmen were killed, and a third warrior had his arm severed. Finding themselves outnumbered and outgunned, the Osage warriors retreated into St. Louis where they received protection by Spanish troops until the other Indians finally returned home.

Before this incident the Missouria warriors had slipped down to Sainte Genevieve and across to Kaskaskia on the British side to steal horses. Spanish and British authorities each captured one of the raiders and gave him a severe thrashing. The Spanish held their prisoner in jail, and when another Missouria came to visit him, they jailed him as well. Lieutenant Governor Piernas ordered all trade with the Missouria and Little Osage suspended "to reduce them to reason." Yet Piernas worried that his actions might bring retaliation or give the Missouria and Little Osage more incentive to trade with the British.

On August 21, 1772, however Unzaga wrote to Piernas recommending harsh treatment of the Missouria and Little Osage.

> There is no other remedy than their extermination since the tolerance which we have had with them, instead of attracting them, has made them insolent. It is clear that the time has arrived when this wrong demands this last sad remedy, but we are not in a position to apply it because [we] lack people and supplies, and lastly because of the expense. You may see, if it is absolutely necessary, that the other nations destroy them, or else may find easier means in which you find no embarrassment.

Unzaga outlined the problem the Spanish had in controlling the Indians of Louisiana Territory. They lacked the resources to pacify the tribes economically or to subjugate them militarily. The Spanish had the same problem in using other tribes as mercenaries to destroy the Missouria and Little Osage. They lacked the economic resources necessary to buy their services. As a result Spain lacked reliable Indian allies in the St. Louis district. Farther south, in the Arkansas Post and Natchitoches districts, the Spanish had stronger ties with the Quapaw and Caddoan tribes. However, these small tribes did not have the military power to deliver a major blow against the Missouria and Osage. The Missouria and Little Osage continually harassed the Spanish though very few deaths occurred. Governor Unzaga wrote to Lieutenant Governor de Meziere at Natchitoches in December of 1772, authorizing him to completely destroy the Osage and Missouria. Unzaga added that the extermination should take place "without cost to the royal treasury." Once again, a Spanish official negated his own policy by setting impossible conditions.

A few months later, on March 19, 1773, Unzaga countermanded his approval to wage war on the Missouria and Osages. Piernas asked Unzaga what he should do with the Missouria horse raiders captured the previous year. Unzaga believed that gentle treatment would restore the friendship of the Missouria and that jail had been an adequate sentence for the two warriors. He directed Piernas to make the Missouria tribe pay for the damages they had caused in St. Louis and to warn them that if they committed future depredations, they would suffer "exemplary punishment." Piernas wrote to Hugh Lord, the commandant of British Illinois on February 21, 1773, explaining actions he had taken the previous year. "It is advisable to inform you that, since certain tribes of the Missouri district (among others those of the Little Osages and the Missouris) having committed repeated attacks, even murders among the inhabitants of my jurisdiction, I decided to deprive them of every sort of supplies by not sending them a single trader so that I might bring them to conciliation." Piernas futilely expected Lord to prevent British traders from entering Spanish territory.

In October or November of 1772, Jean Marie Ducharme, a French trader working for the British, secretly entered the Missouri River with two large boatloads of trade goods. His party slipped past Fort San Carlos at the mouth of the river in the dead of night and proceeded upriver to present-day Saline County. At this time the Little Osage had two villages on the river and Ducharme established his base in the lower village, where he carried on a brisk trade the next four or five months. A headman called Lacorne, a French name, threatened Ducharme, saying if they did not get a trader his people "would strip him of his goods; that his soldiers were angry; that he should take pity on them; that he should give them a little gunpowder to obtain food." The following day Ducharme sent Pierre Bissonet and another engagé to the upper Little Osage and Missouria villages. Bissonet reported that he "saw bands of Great Osages and Missouris coming to trade." The English trade goods included gunpowder, guns, bullets, knives, axes, cloth, blankets, awls, scissors, brass and copper kettles, and a variety of miscellaneous decorative goods such as beads, rings, jewelry, and vermilion.

Word of Ducharme's presence reached St. Louis in February 1773. Lieutenant Governor Piernas was alarmed and sent about one hundred militiamen under Pierre Laclede to arrest Ducharme. The militia had several swivel guns (small cannons) mounted on their canoes. Piernas instructed Laclede to treat the Missouria and Little Osage with kindness. Laclede was to send one of his interpreters to the Missouria with "two porcelain necklaces [white wampum beads] and two calumets of peace." These were universal signs of friendship and would demonstrate to the Missouria the peaceful intent of Laclede's party. Furthermore, if the Missouria assisted in capturing Ducharme and then came to St. Louis to promise good behavior, they would receive presents; trade would resume; and the two Missouria prisoners would be released from jail. The Spanish wanted to approach the Missouria first to get them to mediate with the more aggressive and dangerous Little Osage.

If the Indians resisted and refused to turn over Ducharme, Laclede was authorized to fire on them. On March 11, the Spanish militia made camp near "Isla del Buey" (Island of the Bull) just upstream from present-day Washington, Missouri. Ducharme's party came around the river bend in their canoes and spotted the militia camp. They landed on the opposite bank and took up defensive positions. The militia fired a volley from their guns, and Ducharme's party returned fire; however, all thirteen of his men surrendered when the Spanish promised them amnesty. One of Ducharme's men was an Iroquois warrior, who at first stood fast with him, but one of Laclede's men could speak Iroquois and persuaded the man to surrender. A Little Osage warrior with the group fled and spread word to his tribesmen and the Missouria that a Spanish armada was coming to destroy them. Ducharme fled into the woods, abandoning his peltries, merchandise, and employees to the Spanish authorities. The booty taken from Ducharme included bear skins, deer skins, buffalo robes, grease, tallow and dried meat, dried squash, and some "munitions of war" not yet traded to the Indians.

The Spanish show of force had a profound effect on the Missouria. A trader descending from the Kansa Nation passed the Gumbo Point village unaware of what had happened. The trader reported to Piernas that "the tribe of Missouri Indians was scared . . . their Chief and others were ready to come down to beg mercy and to give satisfaction for the stealing of horses (which they had already gathered up to return). They did not do this promptly because they feared being attacked by other tribes en route to St. Louis." The trader stayed with the Missouria for three days, and they did not molest him or his bales of peltries. When his party departed, the Missouria escorted them a safe distance past the Little Osage villages, which showed signs of hostility. The Missouria and the Big Osage gave evidence of submission by promising to deliver the leader of a war party that had murdered some hunters on the Arkansas River in 1772.

Piernas reported in April of 1773 that the Missouria and the Little Osage were being constantly harassed by enemy nations. The Spanish had encouraged these raids, most of which were carried out by Sac, Fox, Ioway, and, occasionally, even distant Ho Chunk and Potawatomie warriors. These tribes received a steady supply of guns, powder, and lead from the British traders. The Missouria sent word to St. Louis they would come only when these hostile tribes withdrew from the field.

That same month the Spanish government negotiated a truce with the Big Osage that would last until 1777. But the Missouria and Little Osage had again resumed their horse-stealing raids on St. Louis and Sainte Genevieve. By the summer of 1773, harassment of the Little Osage by the other Indian nations was so bad they temporarily fled to the Osage River. The Missouria may have accompanied them. The Big Osage honored their agreement with the Spanish government by refusing sanctuary to their kinsmen, the Little Osage. Spanish traders were coming to their villages, and the Big Osage did not want that trade suspended. They told the Missouria and Little Osage to stop their raids and go talk peace in St. Louis.

Missouria and Little Osage leaders met in August with Spanish officials, who pardoned three warriors for the murder of the three Frenchmen in 1772. A formal agreement was reached with the Missouria and Little Osage stating, "Whoever of these villages henceforth kills some vassal of his Catholic Majesty will be delivered up to the commandant of this post [St. Louis] . . . and punished by death without remission or compassion." The treaty applied equally to Europeans, except in the case of self-defense, when they could kill an Indian without repercussions. All property stolen by the Indians was to be returned in equal value. The treaty ceremony concluded with both parties smoking the sacred pipe and the Spanish giving presents to the Indians. Governor Unzaga rightfully concluded the peace would be valid only in the St. Louis District. To the Missouria and Osage way of thinking, peace was indeed made for St. Louis, but not for all of Spanish territory. St. Louis merchants were very happy as the agreement meant they could profit from the Indian trade again. It did not concern them if Osage and Missouria raids continued against their competitors in the Arkansas Post or Natchitoches districts.

The Spanish, unlike the French, had actually ended the practice of Europeans buying and selling Indian captives for slaves in Louisiana by 1770. Even though slave raiding had ended, the Indians still took prisoners in war. In the spring of 1777, the Sac and Fox captured ten Missouria prisoners in a raid. The new lieutenant governor, Francisco Cruzat, wrote to Commandant de Rocheblave at Fort Gage in British Illinois on June 12, 1777:

> Sir: The general welfare which I believe will result from having peace made between the tribes of the Little Osages and Misuris [Missouria] of the dependency of my government and the Sacs and Renards [Fox] who are located in your district, compels me to give you advice that I am disposed to send an express to these latter tribes to obtain and get from them ten Misuris whom they made prisoners last spring.

Rocheblave provided Cruzat with a letter of support and a passport to enter British territory. When Governor Don Bernardo Galvez's envoy reached the Sac and Fox villages, English traders there accused the Spanish of attempting to lure the tribes into their sphere of influence. The envoy succeeded in ransoming four of the Missouria and a Peoria, who was sent to his tribe at Cahokia as a sign of Spanish good faith. The Missouria met several of their kinsmen in St. Louis and immediately departed for home. The Sac and Fox held the other prisoners, saying they wanted the Missouria and Little Osage leaders to come to their village and smoke the pipe with them. Galvez did not know if the peace council happened, but he believed that the Indians were so warlike that if one tribe stole a horse from another on a whim any peace would be "entirely broken."

Augustin Grignon, a trader at Green Bay, Wisconsin, said that the Wisconsin tribes, especially the Ottawa and Sacs, "were in the habit of making captives of Pawnees, Osages and Missourias. . . ." Grignon personally knew three Osages and two Missouria held as captives. In some cases they had been treated poorly, but he observed that after a while some were given their freedom.

Cruzat prepared a report on November 15, 1777, for Governor Galvez outlining the status of Indian nations that annually received presents in St. Louis. A copy of his report survives in the Missouri History Museum archives in St. Louis:

MISURIS

This tribe is composed of two hundred warriors. The name of the principal chief of this tribe is Kaige, and their location is on the very shores of the Misury river, distant about eighty-six or eighty-seven leagues from this village [St. Louis] Their occupation has always been, and is, that of the hunt; for although they generally plant a small quantity of maize each year, it is not sufficient even for their own support. This tribe is hostile to all the tribes of the Misisipy, and under the same circumstances that we have mentioned when speaking of the Little Osages, The work of hunting in which they are occupied is sufficiently profitable for the trade of this post, as is witnessed by the fact that they annually produce 80 or 90 packs of furs. The only harm experienced from the people of this tribe is the theft of a few horses from the inhabitants of this district, although not so frequently as the case with the Little Osages; and the detaining of the traders who ascend the river for the sole purpose of getting some guns, powder, bullets and other things from them.

This report indicates that the Missouria population had rebounded to around 1,000 people. They were still trying to control the flow of guns and ammunition going upriver. Cruzat estimated the Little Osage at 300 to 350 warriors for a total population between 1,200 and 1,750. He placed their villages a half-league (1.5 miles) inland from the Missouria's. Cruzat noted at this time the Ioway were hostile to the tribes on the Missouri, as were the Sac and Fox. However, he said the latter two tribes "never harmed Spanish interests and they have aided and protected them whenever it has been necessary," suggesting they would attack the Missouria and Little Osage at Spain's bidding.

Cruzat also reported in 1777 that the Big Osages provided St. Louis with 369 packs of tanned deerskin, 122 packs of untanned deer skins, 12 packs of beaver pelts, 41 packs of bear skins, 8 packs of wildcat skins, and 1 pack of otter pelts. The Little Osages produced 146 packs of tanned deer skins, 4 packs of beaver pelts, 3 packs of bear skins, and 1 pack of wildcat skins. The Missouria produced 80 packs of tanned deer skins, 1 pack of beaver pelts, and 2 packs of bear skins. Each pack weighed about 100 pounds. The Osage and Missouria peltries accounted for nearly 60 percent of the profits in the St. Louis fur trade.

The merchants and traders at Arkansas Post and Natchitoches were still reeling under Big Osage raids. The Missouria and Little

Osage resumed horse stealing in the St. Louis District. Agricultural production was threatened due to the loss of horses to the raiders. On March 28, 1779, the citizens of St. Louis and Sainte Genevieve petitioned Lieutenant Governor Leyba to stop the plundering by the Missouria and Little Osage. He did not forward the petition to New Orleans until July.

Leyba pardoned Big Osage warriors for murdering three Frenchmen on the Arkansas River in 1778, calling it "an old matter." He hoped that the tribe would respond to his kind gesture with "good behavior." Government officials generally viewed the hunters and *engagés* from Arkansas Post as low-class. The Spanish, like the French, were inclined to allow the killing of such people by the Osage and Missouria without repercussion as long as the citizens of St. Louis were not harmed and the overall fur trade was not disrupted.

However the horse stealing in the St. Louis district became intolerable. Responding to a citizens' petition, Governor Galvez in New Orleans threatened to shut off all trade to the Missouria and Little Osage, as his predecessors had done. The merchants of St. Louis pressured the government not to take any action; closing the trade would ruin them financially. These measures only pushed the Missouria and Little Osage to trade with the British, who were now operating openly in the Ioway Territory just to their north.

Leyba made it clear that the Little Osage and the Missouria were becoming less important than the Big Osage. He estimated warrior strength as 150 Missouria and 300 Little Osage. The Big Osage had around 1,200 men who could menace Spanish interests or enhance them economically, and their sheer numbers meant Leyba paid more attention to them. He probably also knew the Missouria relationship with the Big Osage was less cordial than that with the Little Osage.

The American Revolution introduced profound changes in the Spanish territory. Spain supported the Americans, and, in retaliation, Britain armed nearly a thousand Indian warriors from the upper Mississippi valley to attack St. Louis on May 16, 1780. The attack failed after a brief siege in which 18 residents were killed, 6 wounded and 57 captured. The Missouria and the Little Osage were not participants in this battle either as friends or foes of Spain. The Treaty of Paris concluded the war on September 3, 1783, and the British Illinois Country became American territory.

The threat of British traders entering Spanish territory from Illinois was eliminated. The British now concentrated their operations at Prairie du Chien, Wisconsin. Many tribes traveled directly to Prairie

Haw-che-ke-su-ga He Who Kills the Osages. This portrait was painted by
George Catlin at Fort Leavenworth, Kansas, in 1832. Catlin thought the
Missouria were in a more "primitive and natural state" than many other
tribes in the area. He described Haw-che-ke-su-ga as "the aged chief of
whom I have spoken and shall yet say more." Unfortunately his remarks
cannot be located. A survivor of the devastating Sac and Fox attack in the
1790s, he signed treaties in 1830, 1833, and 1836. He wears an otter skin tur-
ban, presidential peace medal, and grizzly bear claw necklace, and he holds
a sacred pipe bearing the image of a bear guardian spirit. (Courtesy of the
Smithsonian Museum of American Art, gift of Mrs. Joseph Harrison)

du Chien or even Fort Malden in Canada for gifts and trade goods. British traders also operated directly in the Ioway villages on the Des Moines. For a time, the Ioway refrained from warfare and carried English trade goods directly to the Missouri River tribes. Spanish attempts to evict the English were feeble and usually elicited laughter and scorn from British traders and Indians alike.

On December 12, 1785, Lieutenant Governor Miro issued a report on the status of the tribes along the Missouri River. "The Cances [Kansa] have 200 warriors. . . . They maintain peace with the Little Osages and with the Missouris and make war on the Panis [Pawnee] in order to obtain horses." Confrontations between the Spanish and the Little Osage and Missouria seldom resulted in bloodshed, but fear of the Indians was so strong that the death of even one European sent settlements into panic. In 1787, Louis Lorimier, a trader to the Delaware and Shawnee on the Wabash River, was given a land grant near present-day New Madrid, Missouri, and encouraged to invite those tribes to the Sainte Genevieve District. Spain wanted them as a buffer between their settlements and the Osage and Missouria.

The mention of the Missouria in Spanish records decreases significantly in the last quarter of the eighteenth century. The importance of the Missouria to the fur trade was rapidly decreasing. Populations of fur-bearing animals on the lower Missouri River were being depleted. Fur traders were looking upstream to the Ponca, Arikara, and various Sioux nations for trade. Years of intermittent epidemics and constant warfare with the Sac and Fox were wearing the Missouria down, forcing them to tie their actions ever more closely to those of the Little Osage and Kansa. The Missouria were one warrior society among many, and they were forced to compete for trade and shrinking hunting grounds. Warfare affected their population, but they were not going to give up their homeland easily. Fighting with the Sac and Fox had gone on since around 1700, but now their rivals were gaining the upper hand owing to a steady supply of British guns and munitions. The Sac and Fox had also been spared some of the epidemics that struck the Missouria, giving them much larger numbers.

In 1788 the traders to the Missouria, Little Osage, and Kansa reported a good business and peace prevailing along the Missouri River. However, new problems surfaced for the Spanish government in St. Louis. Besides British traders from Canada reaching the Missouri tribes, unlicensed American traders from Illinois now began going up the Missouri River to trade with the Indians. Other Americans moved into Spanish Illinois, swore loyalty to Spain, and received land grants, pushing the boundary of Euro-American settlement beyond St. Louis, Sainte Genevieve, and New Madrid.

Americans living outside the established settlements presented new temptations to the Missouria, Little Osage, and also the Potawatomie. Governor Miro wanted Lieutenant Governor Perez to protect the new American settlers from the horse-stealing raids of the Missouria by threatening the Indians with harsh measures, then treating them with gentleness and kindness to foster good relations. The Osages were pardoned for "past sins" if they promised to behave themselves in the future. The Indians, long familiar with the stick-and-carrot approach, knew how to exploit it to obtain gifts. Perez was instructed to prevent British and American traders from entering Spanish territory. Spanish Illinois was now threatened on three sides: by the British in the north, by the Americans in the east, and by the Missouria and Osage in the west. To make matters worse, Napoleon Bonaparte expressed interest in reacquiring the Louisiana Territory for France.

The Spanish hoped to gain Osage and Missouria support against further British, American, and now possible French encroachment. They failed miserably. Perez suspended trade with the Big and Little Osages. On November 8, 1791, he reported that traders were heading upriver with goods intended for the Missouria and Kansa nations. The Big Osage robbed the traders and threatened worse if future goods were not delivered to them instead. In March of 1792, Perez wanted another boatload of trade goods sent to the Missouria and Kansa to keep them from seeking out British traders established on the Des Moines River.

Carl Chapman suggested that Perez's directive meant the Missouria had joined the Kansa at this point. However, some traders were awarded licenses to trade with more than one tribe. On March 11, 1784, the Sarpy brothers of St. Louis received a license to trade with both the Kansa and Missouria, while a man named Sanguinet received a license to trade with the Little Osage. Henri Peyroux de la Coudreniere, the military and civil commandant of Sainte Genevieve, received a license to trade with the Missouria in 1790, but not with the Kansa or Little Osage. It is possible that the Missouria were hunting with the Kansa in the winter of 1791–1792 to avoid the Sac and Fox.

Reports of events unfolding in the 1790s do not directly mention the Missouria. However, as allies of the Little Osage and because of their location on the Missouri River, they were certainly affected. Lieutenant Governor Perez wrote to Louis Lorimier on May 4, 1792, "I have done all I could to excite the Sacs and Renards [Foxes] to go to war with them [Osages]. At my request several parties have gone into their country and at this moment I learn that one such party has returned after killing five persons." In December of 1792, the governor issued orders that a general attack was to be made on the Osages as enemies of Spain. On May 1, 1793, Lieutenant Governor Zenon Trudeau directed Lorimier to have the "Loups" (Delaware) and "Chavauesnons" (Shawnee) join the attack. A trade embargo was imposed on the Osages in conjunction with the military action in the belief "they will certainly come to their senses."

Despite the objections of St. Louis merchants, trade was suspended to all the tribes on the Missouri for fear that the Osages would simply rob the traders of whatever they needed, defeating the purpose of the embargo. On the northern frontier, hostile Ioway and Sac and Foxes were blocking the Osages from reaching British traders on the Des Moines River, even though the English wanted the Osage business. The Spanish encouraged the three tribes to prevent English traders from making their way to the Missouri River. As a result, the Sac, Fox, and Ioway were able to pit the Spanish and English against each other and receive presents and generous terms of trade from both sides.

On June 2, 1793, Lieutenant Governor Trudeau made it clear to the Indians and Spanish citizens of Louisiana that war against the Osages was declared and it was necessary to close trade to all tribes on the Missouri River. Trudeau said the Spanish government was depriving itself of an "important trade" in order to use the resources to arm the various tribes "who have been insulted and outraged" by the Osages. The governor hoped, at the very least, that the Osages would be driven far away, leaving their territory in the hands of tribes more compliant to the whims of the Spanish government.

The Spanish recruited not only the Ioway and Sac and Fox in the north; they sought the aid of small bands of Delaware, Shawnee, Abnaki, Ottawa, Miami, Piankeshaw, Quapaw, Caddo, Chickasaw, and Cherokee who had settled in the Sainte Genevieve and Arkansas Districts. Armed with British guns, the Sac and Fox and Ioway drove the more poorly armed Kansa from the Missouri River onto the plains farther west. They then turned their attention to the Little Osage and Missouria.

In the meantime, French Minister Edmond Charles Genêt had arrived in America. Following Napoleon's wish to reclaim Louisiana, Genêt tried to assemble an invasion force on the Ohio River. Lieutenant Governor Baron de Carondelet in St. Louis feared the French would receive open support from 1,200 Osage and Missouria warriors and would take all of Spanish Illinois "while the inhabitants were occupied driving back or receiving attacks from the French army of Genet." Pacane, a Miami warrior, admitted that Spain's Indian allies were saying, "Our Father the Frenchman is coming. As soon as we shall see him, we shall escape to him." However, Genêt's threatened invasion failed to materialize.

Auguste and Pierre Chouteau convinced the Spanish authorities in St. Louis that if they received exclusive trade rights for the Big and Little Osages, they could persuade them to stop raiding and disrupting the fur trade. The Chouteau brothers knew the Osage well; family members had married into the Big Osage tribe. They received their six-year contract on May 18, 1794, and made good on their promise. Spain's Indian allies were told to disband and go home. A disgusted Pacane told Lorimier, "How . . . is it possible for the savage tribes to be steadfast and tranquil? The interests of the whites is the sole cause of it [the war] From the first to the last, the Commandants love money so much they beg us and they drag us to places which they see to be favorable to their interests?" Intertribal warfare and feuds had gone on for generations, but as Pacane's words show, European meddling had increased their frequency and intensity. This warfare, coupled with disease, had ground the Missouria down.

On December 2, 1795, Baron de Carondelet wrote a summary of the recent war for Don Luis de las Casas, governor general of Cuba. Carondelet identified the Little Osage as living on the Osage River near the Big Osage villages. He boasted, "I incited the other savages, their neighbors to make raids against them—engaging the latter [Little Osage], by presents and the distribution of arms, to wage war more actively against both."

Peace came too late to save the Missouria. The Missouria had played a strong role for years in attacking the Fox and forcing their merger with the Sac. The Missouria, in effect, had been waging a war with the Sac and Fox within a war between two imperial powers: Spain and the Osage. Consequently, the Sac and Fox had motives for attacking the Missouria that were separate from Spanish interests. In addition to the munitions they got from British traders, they had received guns, powder, and lead from the Spanish. William Clark wrote on June 15, 1804, "The war was so hot fierce & both nations become so reduced the Little Osage & and a few Missouris moved and built a village 5 miles near the Grand Osages, the rest of the Missouries went and took protection under the Otteaus [Otoes] on the Platte River." Unfortunately, Clark left the time of this departure blank in his notes.

When Maximilian met the Missouria in 1833, he reported, "This tribe was formerly numerous and powerful, but being defeated by the Foxes, Saukies and Osages, it lost its independence and the few that remain have intermingled with the Otos." He recorded the most graphic account of the calamity that befell the tribe:

> We were at the part called Fox Prairie, the Saukie and Fox Indians, and, perhaps, some other nations, formerly attacked, and nearly extirpated the tribe of the Missouris. The remainder of the people saved themselves among the Otos . . . where their descendants still live. . . . The Missouris came down the river in many canoes, and their enemies had concealed themselves in the willow thickets. After the Missouris, who suspected no evil, had been killed or wounded with arrows, the victors leaped into the water, and finished their bloody work with clubs and knifes; very few of the Missouris escaped.

Fox Prairie on his map corresponds roughly with the Pettisaw Plains of northern Saline County. Maximilian's account followed the actual events by about forty years, and he did not say who related them to him, though possibly it was Indian agent John Dougherty.

In 1920 Milford Chandler made wax-cylinder recordings of war bundle stories handed down and told by an aged Ho Chunk man named Mark Green. Mr. Green's paternal grandfather, Black Otter, had accompanied a war party as a young boy. According to Black Otter, a party of Ho Chunk and Sac went to war against the Osage. They attacked a large village on an island in the Missouri River. The inhabitants tried to escape in canoes but were killed or captured. The warriors celebrated their victory until they learned a woman taken captive "spoke their own language." She told them this village had been out hunting. Black Otter said the woman was a "Nu djatci," which is close in pronunciation to Nyut^achi. To their dismay, the

warriors learned that they had attacked a village of the Missouria—
"their own people" or kinsmen. This error apparently did not matter
to their Sac allies.

While the account is similar to Maximilian's, it is difficult to pin-
point where or when this event occurred. Black Otter's birth was
estimated to be around 1782, and he was possibly fourteen at the
time, which would make the year 1796. In oral tradition, however, a
timeline can be off by several years. The narrative indicates that the
site was downstream from the Little Osage village. The explanation
of the captured woman seems to make it clear this was a clan hunting camp rather than a main Missouria village. Though Black Otter's
party expressed remorse over attacking their distant kinsmen, the
Ho Chunk previously had gone to war against the Missouria. In 1746
Ho Chunk and Menominee warriors had raided the Missouria. Again
in 1751, "a numerous band of Puants [Winnebago] went on the war-
path against the Missouris at the beginning of the month of March."
They left without the knowledge of Sieur Pierre Marin, the commandant at Green Bay, in Wisconsin. This time a Menominee headman
called "la Mothe" helped Marin stop several other Ho Chunk war
parties that had formed that spring to attack the Missouria.

Complicating the chronology of attacks on the Missouria, William
Clark reported the existence of an "ancient" Missouria village on
June 13, 1804, which does not coincide with the Gumbo Point, Utlaut
or the Utz site. This passage is from the 1814 edition of the *Journals of
Lewis and Clark* edited by Nicolas Biddle:

> We passed at between four and five miles, a bend of the river, and
> two creeks on the north, called the Round Bend creeks. Between
> these two creeks is the prairie, in which once stood the ancient vil-
> lage of the Missouris. Of this village there remains no vestige, nor
> is there any thing to recall this great and numerous nation, except
> the feeble remnants of about thirty [eighty in original notes] fami-
> lies. They were driven from their original seats by the invasions of
> the Sauks and other Indians from the Mississippi, who destroyed
> at this village two hundred [three hundred in original notes] of
> them in one contest, and sought refuge near the Little Osage, on
> the other side of the river. The encroachment of the same enemies
> forced, about thirty years since, both these nations from the banks
> of the Missouri. A few retired with the Osage, and the remainder
> found an asylum on the river Platte among the Ottoes, who are
> themselves declining.

A portion of a mural from Missouri's American Indian Cultural Center at Van Meter State Park. This shows the Missouria village on the Pinnacles of the Utz site as it might have appeared about 1673. The dwellings are the chakiruthan (house tied together) the prairie mat lodge. The "Old Fort" is visible in the background. Despite the large size of the Utz site, it is evident that the entire site was not occupied at a single time. Intermittent occupation may have occurred as late as the 1720s. (Courtesy of the Missouri Department of Natural Resources)

This location is in Chariton County on an old channel of the Missouri River near Dalton. There is some speculation that this was the site of the Black Otter incident. Given the fact that the Missouria had been at war with the Sac and Fox for decades, it is probable that there was more than one devastating attack on the tribe. The Black Otter war party's attack appears to me to have been one in a series as opposed to the "final blow" that forced them to flee to the Otoe.

On June 11, the Corps of Discovery met a party of traders coming downriver from the "Sioux country." Among them was an old French trapper named Dorian, who had lived among the Missouri River tribes for nearly twenty-five years. Dorian was persuaded to accompany the expedition to help establish relations with the Yankton and Teton Sioux. Clark probably received his information about the Missouria village and the battle from Dorian. However, maps

prior to Clark's time generally show the Missouria villages in the approximate location of the Pinnacles or Pettisaw Plains.

Although locals have collected native materials in the vicinity, so
far no Oneota or historic period Indian site has been officially recorded in this location. On June 15, the Corps of Discovery camped
across the river from the Gumbo Point and Plattner village sites. Clark
wrote the Missourias had fled here and "resided under the protection of the Osages after their nation was reduced by the Saukees at
their town some distance below." An entry by Bourgmont on April
30, 1714, locates the Missouria village past "another little island and
some small trees, above which we can see the village situated on a
beautiful prairie to the west. . . ." This can be interpreted as "over the
tops" or "upstream" from the small trees. Consequently, it appears
that at least a majority of the Missouria were then living at or near
the Gumbo Point site. The Utz site would not have been very visible,
as it was half a mile from the river and mostly on the back slope of
the Pinnacles.

Philip La Renudiere reported in 1723 that the Missouria lived in
"100 shacks" on the south bank of the Missouri River at the place
now identified as Gumbo Point. Trader James Mackay described this
area in 1797 as "Two old villages of Little Osage and Missouria . . .
upon the south bank, on a beautiful and very high plain: these two
nations were forced to abandon this place because of constant war
between them and the nations of the Mississippi."

Based on the limited evidence, it seems likely that the Missouria
were compelled by Sac and Fox attacks to move from the Utz site,
or an unknown site, to Gumbo Point, effectively putting the Little
Osage between them and their enemies. Perhaps Dorian or Clark had
been confused about the original location of the Missouria village.
However, Dorian certainly had firsthand knowledge of the area and
its inhabitants, and Clark's journals are usually quite reliable.

In October 2009, National Park Service archaeologists Andrew
Veech and Steve DeVore undertook an investigation of the Chariton
County site near Dalton. University of Missouri geographer James
Harlan pinpointed the site based on Clark's journals. The Otoe-
Missouria tribal government, which was interested in recovering
their history, sanctioned the project. Magnetometery surveys (ground
sonar) of the location were conducted. Readings indicated disturbed
earth in geometric patterns and what appear to be fire pits within
lodge outlines, all consistent with Native American activity. No sur-

face artifacts were found, but the site has been covered by four to five feet of sediment. Although results are promising, more investigation is needed to determine if this was indeed a Missouria village. (About a dozen tribal elders visited Missouri for two days in October 2009 to learn more about the archeological investigation and their ancestral homeland. I gave a group, mostly from the Pigeon Clan a tour of the Utz, Plattner, Gumbo Point, and Arrow Rock sites. I also shared my original research for this book and showed the group some of the maps and images that are reproduced in it. The staff of Van Meter State Park demonstrated the programs given to schoolchildren about Missouria history and culture. The elders seemed genuinely pleased with these efforts to preserve and interpret this early chapter of their history. At the Dalton site, Lorena DeRoin, the oldest living member of the tribe, made an impassioned plea about the need to preserve their heritage and pass it on to younger generations. A prayer was said for the archaeologists in their search, and sacred cedar and sacred earth was collected at the site to take back to Red Rock, Oklahoma.)

The 1814 edition of the journals of Lewis and Clark indicates the Missouria left the Dalton site about thirty years before joining the Otoe, placing the last date of occupation around 1764. This fits the time frame when the Missouria fled to Illinois to escape attacks from the Big Osage. Some secondary sources indicate the Osage pushed the Missouria to the north bank of the river. If this is correct, the Missouria may have fled from Gumbo Point to the Dalton site. After Laclede persuaded them to leave St. Louis, they could have returned to the Dalton site. The devastating attack by the Sac and Fox, reported by Clark, could have forced them to make peace with the Osage and return to the Gumbo Point site.

Manuscripts from Kaskaskia dating between 1736 and 1742 discuss traders going to the "Post of the Missouris" to trade with the Indians residing there. This installation postdates Fort Orleans by eight years and predates Fort Cavagnial by two years. There are no details of where it was or who operated it. If it were a new post in the Dalton area instead of a reactivated Fort Orleans, the Missouria may have relocated nearby. The Dalton site could be a temporary village, a hunting camp, or an early village not known to mapmakers. Lieutenant Governor Pedro Piernas wrote on January 4, 1771, that the Missouria and Little Osage are "about 85 leagues" up the Missouri River, but "their villages are not always fixed," indicating some relocation of villages occurred. The site could also be a Native American site predating the Oneota or Missouria occupation, or it could simply be a case of mistaken identity.

Curiously, no contemporary Spanish accounts of the final demise and departure of the Missouria have been found. Perhaps no Europeans witnessed this massacre, or, if they did, they did not survive to tell about it. However, it seems possible that such a document has either been destroyed or still awaits discovery in some Spanish archive. Many pieces of Missouria history are missing and remain a matter of speculation pending further research.

The question remains: exactly when did this final catastrophe befall the Missouria? William Clark omitted that information from his field journals. Various authors have listed dates, ranging from 1789 to 1798. A map drawn in 1795 by Antoine Soulard in St. Louis does not show any Missouria or Little Osage villages on the Missouri River, but Jacques Clamorgan of the Missouri Company recorded the "Abode of the Otoes and Missouris at the entrance of the River Platte" on a hand drawn map in September 1796. Jean Baptist Truteau wrote in 1795 that on the right bank of the Missouri "six leagues [21 miles] farther up [from the Grand River] have been living *since several years ago* the nations of the Missouri and the Little Osages. The former have been almost entirely destroyed by the nations situated on the Mississippi. The latter took refuge higher up on the Great Osage River." The accounts of both Clark and Truteau seem to indicate that the Missouria and Little Osage departed from the Missouri River about the same time.

We know that in 1791 a pirogue of trade goods was sent to the Missouria. In March of 1792, a second pirogue was ordered to go to the Missouria. In November of 1791, Lieutenant Governor Perez had reported a worrisome development. The Osage and Sac were at peace, and large numbers of them had been seen hunting together on the Missouri River. This détente between the two powerful nations could have lulled the Missouria into letting their guard down. By May of 1792, the Spanish were actively inciting the Sac and Fox against the Osage. The account of the Sac and Fox, wading in the Missouri River to attack the canoes, suggests the season was summer or early fall, when water was usually low. The Missouria may have been preparing to travel to St. Louis, returning from hunting with the Kansa, or preparing to move their whole village when they were struck. The Sac and Fox knew the patterns of Missouria travel. Low-water conditions and the détente between the Sac, Fox, and the Osage followed by Spanish incitement of war could have enhanced the time for an all-out attack on the Missouria in 1792 or 1793. These approximate dates seem to coincide well with the report by Truteau.

This final blow, when it fell, was devastating and totally demoralized the surviving Missouria. Out of some eight hundred people, perhaps half survived. The tribe that seventy years earlier had prevented French expeditions and traders from going up the Missouri River unchecked was finished as an independent nation. The blood feud between the Missouria and Fox initiated at Detroit in 1712 had come full circle. Survivors could not agree on the next course of action and they scattered. William Clark reported about thirty families living with the Otoes in 1804. Government agent George C. Sibley wrote in 1820 that twenty families of Missouria still lived with the Little Osage on the Neosho River. Edwin James reported four or five Missouria families living with the Kansa in 1819. Some Missouria apparently left the Otoes and joined the Ioway, at least temporarily. Even in this disrupted and depleted state, the Missouria did not completely disappear. Once again, they reconstituted what they could of their clan structures. They were still recognized as Missouria and maintained their own leaders within their host tribes. Small parties of Missouria undoubtedly still entered parts of their old domain in Missouri to hunt or to visit the graves of their ancestors, a practice common among many Indian tribes.

5

The Americans

Rapid and Dramatic Change

On March 9, 1804, at a ceremony in St. Louis, the Spanish flag was lowered and the French flag raised and then lowered. The next day the American flag rose in its place. These ceremonies formally marked the official passing of Louisiana Territory from Spain to France in 1800 and from France to the United States in 1803. Once again the native people were not consulted regarding a foreign power claiming jurisdiction; they were merely informed. For over 130 years, the American Indians of Upper Louisiana had felt the impact of the presence of Europeans and their manufactured trade goods. The French and Spanish occupied little land and usually stayed close to the major rivers. The Missouria had accepted trade goods without accepting European culture, and the trade items obtained were adapted to fit into their culture. The arrival of the Americans would change their culture more quickly and in ways that no one, Indian or white, could have imagined at the time.

On May 14, 1804, Captain Meriwether Lewis and his co-commander, William Clark, started their "Voyage of Discovery" to explore the Missouri River and find the fabled route to the Pacific Ocean. The expedition traveled six hundred miles before encountering any Indians. On July 28, a short distance above the Platte River, hunter George

As governor of Louisiana Territory, Meriwether Lewis assessed
the disposition of western Indian tribes toward the United States.
He deemed the Missouria friendly but thought that the Otoe were
questionable. He doubted many tribes would remain loyal unless
a trading post was built on the Missouri River. (Courtesy of the
State Historical Society of Missouri)

Druillard met three Missouria hunters skinning an elk. He brought
a Missouria to meet Captains Lewis and Clark. The Missouria man
was the first American Indian to officially meet Lewis and Clark on
their journey. He explained that most of the nation was on the plains
hunting buffalo. His group, composed of twenty families, was encamped four miles away. These were members of the tribe unable to
follow the buffalo hunt because of illness, age, or infirmity.

The following day Clark sent crew member La Liberté and the Missouria to invite the rest of the camp to a council. On the evening of August 2, Sergeant Charles Floyd recorded that six headmen, seven warriors, and a French trader fired guns in greeting as they approached the camp. The expedition's cannon was fired in a return salute. Lewis and Clark presented the Indians with small gifts and tobacco and shook their hands. In return the Indians presented the explorers with watermelons.

After breakfast on the next morning, Clark delivered a long speech informing the Indians about the change in government, the purpose of the expedition, and the way the United States expected the Indians to conduct themselves. Clark reported,

> To the six chiefs who were present, we gave a medal of the second grade to one Ottoe chief, and one Missouri chief; a medal of the third grade to two inferior chiefs of each nation: the customary mode of recognizing a chief, being to place a medal around his neck, which is considered among his tribe as a proof of his consideration abroad. Each of these medals was accompanied by a present of paint, garters, and cloth ornaments of dress; and to this we added a canister of [gun] powder, a bottle of whiskey, and a few presents to the whole. . . . The absent grand chief was an Ottoe named Weahrushhah. . . . Little Thief.

"Shongotongo" (*Sunge xa^nje*), Big Horse, an Otoe, and "Wethea" (Hospitality), a Missouria, were the two leaders receiving medals of the second grade. Clark's meeting took place in an area in present-day Nebraska, "the Council Bluffs." He reported the Indians as "perfectly satisfied" with the gifts and medals. Captain Lewis shot his air gun, which astonished them. Clark sent a medal, some articles of clothing, and an American flag to the absent Little Thief.

On August 18, Otoe and Missouria headmen who had been buffalo hunting caught up with the expedition. Those who met with Lewis and Clark this time were Little Thief, Big Horse, and Otoe headmen Iron Eyes, Big Axe, and Big Blue Eyes (Very Big Eyes), and Missouria headmen "Karkapaha" *Kax'epa*, Crow's Head, and "Nenasawa," Black Cat, (probably *Mingké Thewe*, Black Raccoon). The Indians begged for the pardon of Private Moses Reed, who had been court-martialed and whipped for desertion. Private Joseph Whitehouse reported, "The Indians were all concerned at seeing Reed receive his punishment, and seemed truly sorry."

The following morning Clark noted Big Horse arrived at breakfast naked. Big Horse told Clark that he had to return home naked. Matt Jones, an Otoe-Missouria informant, believes Big Horse's recognition as a "chief" by the explorers in the first council violated tribal protocol. His lesson in humility was to remain naked for the duration of the second council. The explorers made the same speeches and again distributed presents, medals, and commissions. Clark observed that the Indians were not satisfied with the presents. At one point Very Big Eyes gave back his commission. Clark complained that the Indians became very troublesome, begging for whiskey and more presents. In turn, the Otoe and Missouria were not very impressed with the stingy Americans.

The headmen explained that the Omaha had killed two Missouria warriors who were stealing horses, leading to war between the two tribes. They also feared retaliation by the Pawnees from whose villages they had stolen corn while the Pawnees were away on a hunt. Clark wanted them to make peace with their neighbors, and they promised to do so. He estimated that the Otoe and Missouria tribes numbered 250 men, one-third of whom were Missouria. Sergeant Floyd wrote, "The Missouries is a very small nation. The Otoes is a large nation." Clark presented the Indians an extra canister of whiskey and the less-than-satisfactory council was ended.

In November 1804, as the government of Louisiana Territory was undergoing transition, Auguste Chouteau informed Secretary of the Treasury Albert Gallatin of the current state of the Indian trade. Chouteau estimated the annual trade in merchandise going to the Missouria Nation at the equivalent of $4,000 at London prices and double that amount for the Otoes. He estimated the population of Indians in Louisiana by "hombres" (men) for each tribe. These were the able-bodied men capable of hunting and therefore contributing to the fur trade. Chouteau listed 80 Missouria men and 120 Otoe men, making a population of about 320 Missouria and 480 Otoe or 800 in total.

Meriwether Lewis had instructed Indian headmen to send delegates to Washington to meet their new "father," President Thomas Jefferson. On October 21, 1805, General James Wilkinson instructed Captain Amos Stoddard to conduct a delegation of Indian leaders from St. Louis to Washington D.C. Twenty-six leaders of eleven tribes were initially selected for the trip, including Little Thief of the Otoe and two Missouria, to visit the nation's capital. Stoddard was instructed to save government funds by purchasing his own provisions and camping and cooking out along the way. Little Thief died on the trip, but the Missouria apparently completed the journey, the first of their people to visit the nation's capital.

The delegation arrived in Washington around Christmas and created a sensation. Augustus John Foster, a British diplomat wrote,

> Deputies from Eight Nations beyond the Metchisippi [Mississippi] are arrived. They passed on Horseback by my window a few days ago. . . . Two of them were naked to the waist, their Head shaved to the Crown, faces red, Ears green & Feathers & bills of birds stuck all over them. Others had their faces shaded with black & streaks of Black painted from the Crown to the Chin, with Sack loads of Feathers & Quills tied to their hair behind. They are 21 in all generally tall stout men but not so much so as I expected to find them.

Charles Wilson Peale made silhouette portraits of several delegates. Two of the subjects of these portraits, "Macapaba" and "Tahawarra," are tentatively identified in Smithsonian Institution records as Missouria. If they indeed are Missouria, the two images would be the earliest illustrations of tribe members known to exist. However, the portraits may be misidentified or their names incorrectly and poorly transcribed. Some Otoe-Ioway language speakers could not readily translate these names. Other language specialists suggest that Macapaba is an Algonquin name and Tahawarra is Pawnee.

On January 4, 1806, President Jefferson met the Indian leaders and addressed them:

> My friends & children, Chiefs of the Osages, Missouris, Kanzas, Ottos, Panis, Ayowas, & Sioux. I take you by the hand of friendship and give you a hearty welcome to the seat of government of the U.S.
> The French, the English, the Spaniards, have now agreed with us to retire from all the country which you & we hold between Canada and Mexico, and never more to return to it. We are become as numerous as the leaves of the trees and tho' we do not boast, we do not fear any nation. We are now your fathers; and you shall not lose by the change. [Jefferson wanted to impress upon the Indians the dominant position of the United States.]

However, the Indians knew the president's words were not entirely true. British traders from Canada still sold goods to the tribes on

President Thomas Jefferson by George Caleb Bingham. Jefferson
secured the purchase of the Louisiana Territory for the United
States in 1803, placing the Missouria and Otoe under American influence. He met representatives of the Missouria and Otoe nations
in January of 1806. Jefferson wanted the loyalty and friendship of
the Indians, but also initiated policies to separate them from their
land and assimilate them into agrarian white American society.
(Courtesy of the State Historical Society of Missouri)

the Missouri River, and Spanish from New Mexico still traded with
tribes on the Great Plains.

Jefferson expressed his desire to become acquainted with his "red
children" west of the Mississippi and of uniting with them in the
bonds of peace & friendship, "as we have done with those on this
side of that river." Jefferson also promised to furnish them all the
trade goods they wanted in exchange for their furs and peltries, with
no profit being made by the government in the exchange. Jefferson

was not simply being magnanimous with the Indians. He wanted their loyalty, but more than that, he wanted them to become dependent on the government. Jefferson had a plan in mind for later, as he wrote to Meriwether Lewis, "commerce is the great engine by which we are to coerce them & not war." Trade was to be a tool to create indebtedness by the Indians, which they could repay by land cessions. As their land base shrank, the Indians would have to depend more on agriculture and less on hunting, making it easier for them to assimilate into American agrarian society. Jefferson believed this would be a gradual process, occurring over the span of a hundred years. History proved his theory of gradual and peaceful assimilation would not work.

The Indians had heard similar speeches of friendship from the French, the Spanish, and the English for over a century. They formulated a response, which was given through an interpreter the same day. It is not known how much each headman contributed to the speech, and the interpreters could have embellished it. Some of it is very uncharacteristic language for Siouan and Pawnee warriors.

> Speech of the Osages, Missouris, Otos, Panis, Cansas, Ayowais & Sioux Nations to the president of the U.S. & to the Secretary at War. My Grandfather & My Father. It is with an open heart that we receive your hands, friendship stretches ours in yours & unites them together . . . fathers, we have to thank our interpreters who advised us to strengthen our hearts. . . . Our interpreters told us that our fathers were good & would pity us, that they wanted to be acquainted with their new red Children.

The speech implored the president to make sure that traders did not take too many furs for very little goods or they would be no better off than they were now. It restated over and over how happy they were, how worthy of pity they were, and how they no longer wished to fight, but to "shut the mouth of your Children who speak war, stop the arm of those who rise the tomahawk over our heads." Finally they promised the president, "We will keep your Word in our Bosom [heart]."

The speech was probably calculated not to insult their hosts and to gain favor in matters of trade. But despite the talk of peace and friendship, tradition would resume when they went home. The Americans still seemed very far away, and they would deal with them as they had the Europeans before them. But the meeting with Jefferson was a harbinger of change unlike anything they had seen before.

Meriwether Lewis, now governor of Louisiana Territory, informed the secretary of war in July 1808 of the status of the western tribes. The Spanish in New Mexico influenced all the *Kitkehahki*, Republican Pawnee; most of the *Chaui*, Grand Pawnee; *Skidi*, Wolf Pawnee; and the Kansa, Omaha, and Ponca. Only the Big and Little Osages, part of the Grand Pawnee, and the Missouria were considered by Lewis to be loyal to American interests. The standing of the Otoe and *Pitahawiratas*, Tapage Pawnee, was not made known by Lewis. He expressed doubt that those few tribes would remain loyal unless trading posts were established on the Missouri River. His opinion helped lead to the construction of Fort Osage on the Fire Prairie, at present-day Sibley, Missouri, in September of 1808. William Clark had noted the spot was an excellent site for a fort in 1804. A portion of the fort has been reconstructed and is now managed by Jackson County Parks and Recreation.

Fort Osage was constructed in September of 1808 at the "Fire Prairie" (present-day Sibley, Missouri) at the direction of Meriwether Lewis and William Clark. A band of Missouria families, joined to the Little Osage, resided intermittently and traded at the post as late as 1822. Missouria and Otoe from the Platte River also periodically visited the post. The fort has been partially reconstructed by Jackson County Parks and Recreation. (Courtesy of the State Historical Society of Missouri)

Originally named Fort Clark, in honor of William Clark, the military and trading post was the focal point of trade for the Big and Little Osage Indians and was intended to keep them, as well as the Missouria band living with the Little Osage, friendly to the United States. George Champlain Sibley, the government trader or "factor" also traded with the Kansa, and he hoped to acquire trade with the Otoe and Missouria living on the Platte River.

By 1808, many Indians east of the Mississippi River were gathering under the leadership of the Shawnee leader Tecumseh and his brother Tenskawatawa, "the Shawnee Prophet." They were angered by the loss of millions of acres of land through provisions of dubious treaties and the waves of white settlers pouring into the Ohio River valley. Tecumseh wanted to create an alliance of Indian nations from Canada to the Gulf Coast to halt the tide of white settlement encroaching on Indian land. His emissaries traveled throughout the West, imploring the Missouria, Otoe, Osage, Ioway, Sac and Fox, and others to join them before they too lost their lands and way of life.

The United States blamed Great Britain for creating the Indian confederacy. Officials failed to see that it was resentment of American policies that was fueling their actions. The British still wanted the lucrative fur trade of the Indians, and they feared American expansion into Canada. They wanted a sovereign "Indian country" as a buffer between Canada and the United States. The Sac and Fox, Ioway, Ho Chunk, Kickapoo, Ottawa, and Potawatomie received weapons and gunpowder from British traders. However, the British were not yet actively encouraging Indians to attack Americans. That did not stop some of the warriors from attacking isolated settlements. While Indian leaders considered Tecumseh's proposals, the Ioway decided instead to fight their old enemy, the Osage. Newspaper accounts report the Missouria were drawn into this conflict.

The *Hampshire Federalist* in Springfield, Massachusetts, carried a report from George Sibley at Fort Osage dated November 8, 1809:

> On the 4th of this instant a hunting party of the Osage tribe, consisting of five men and four women, crossed the Missouri River, from the fort . . . they were surprised by a party of Ioways who killed one man and two women, and another man is missing, supposed to be killed some distance from their camp. Next morning Captain Clemson with a detachment of fifteen men, Doctor Murray and myself, were conducted to the fatal spot. . . . On the following day a Missouri Indian from the Ioway Village, called over the river for a canoe at the garrison, one of the defeated party

knew him and said he shot at and chased him in the attack . . . Captain Clemson sent for the Missouri Indian and interrogated him closely, suspecting him as a spy . . . he said it was the wish of the Ioways to cover the grave of the dead with presents, and be at peace.

Two Missouria men from a hunting camp on the Kansas River arrived at the fort on February 6, 1811. They had been sent by their headmen to see about settling the tribe at the fort. Sibley estimated there were twenty lodges in the hunting camp and another eight to ten lodges still on the Platte. Sibley showed them his trading house, and they were surprised at the cheap prices of the goods. They thought he was joking, and he directed them to the Little Osage to verify his prices. Complaining of the prices charged by their trader, the Missouria men expected the entire tribe to arrive in spring and thought maybe the Otoe would follow.

In 1811, hostilities involving the Osage, Missouria, and Ioway increased. The Osage were allied to the United States, but most of the Ioway were loyal to Great Britain, leading to a proxy war. On March 12, 1811, Sibley wrote:

> About sunrise another War party set off from the Osage Village against the Ioways of about 45 men consisting of about an equal number of Osages & Missouris, led by a distinguished warrior of the Missouri named Che-o-ho-ge or hole in my house [*Chi ùxoge* = hole in house]. Their plan is to attack the enemy by surprise. . . . Lieut. Brownson set them across the River, and they immediately set out on this march.
>
> The war party returned several days later with 8 scalps and one horse taken from the Ioway.

On June 18, 1812, the United States declared war on Great Britain, citing British naval policies and their arming of the Indians on the frontier as reasons for the action. A group of Indian headmen from numerous tribes, who were visiting Washington D.C. at the time, were told by President James Madison "to sit quietly and watch them [Americans] deliver their red brothers." The official policy of the United States was to maintain the neutrality of Indian tribes. The British however, now openly armed and encouraged Indian tribes to make war on the United States.

On June 26 a council of ten tribes was held at the Sac village of Saukenuk on the Rock River in Illinois. Each participant received a

As an explorer, superintendent of Indian affairs in the West, and governor of Missouri Territory, William Clark treated the Missouria as a semi-independent nation. On August 4, 1826, he wrote in a letter to Mary Easton Sibley: "I had the honor of receiving your letter of the 9th of June by a party of Missouri Indians who pass by your house on their way to this place. The friendly part which you took, in procuring or becoming responsible for a Canoe for those Indians to the Missouri [River] deserves all the grateful feelings which Indians possess, and for which I beg you to accept my thanks." (Courtesy of the State Historical Society of Missouri)

wampum belt tied with red ribbon, a symbol of war, and a sacred pipe to smoke and seal the alliance. Otoe and Missouria warriors were present. A Kickapoo emissary of the Shawnee Prophet exhorted the tribes to join the Indian confederacy and support the British. The Otoe and Missouria replied, "We will receive your wampum and take it to our chiefs—we are only young men and no chiefs." They did not smoke the pipe. The Otoe and Missouria headmen did not change allegiances because they "could make more trapping beaver than making war against the Americans."

Fort Osage was so remote it did not contribute to defense of the frontier settlements and was vulnerable to having its supply line cut. The fort was abandoned in June of 1813 and its garrison sent to other assignments. Sibley constructed a new trading house for the Osage at the Arrow Rock bluff. From October 1813 until April 1814, when the post was abandoned, the Little Osage and the Missouria with them were residing nearby and hunting and trapping in the area.

William Clark, now governor of Missouri Territory, reported in September of 1814 that the British were making "great exertions to win over" the Osage, Kansa, Otoe, Missouria, and Sioux. To offset the military threat to Missouri settlements, St. Louis fur trader and U.S. Indian Agent Manuel Lisa encouraged the Teton Lakota, Ponca, and Omaha to attack the pro-British Ioway and Sac and Fox tribes. The Otoe and Missouria declined Lisa's offer, stating that for them war might be better another time. They had no quarrel with the Ioway at this time, and the Sac and Fox had left them alone because they were busy fighting Americans.

The war between Great Britain and the United States was concluded on December 24, 1814, with a treaty in Ghent, Belgium. It took months for the news to reach the western frontier, however, and a separate peace had to be made with the Indian nations. A peace conference was held with twenty tribes at Portage des Sioux, beginning in July of 1815. On Sept. 12, 1815, the Big and Little Osages signed the treaty affirming their allegiance to the United States:

> A treaty of peace and friendship, made and concluded between William Clark, Ninian Edwards, and Auguste Chouteau, Commissioners Plenipotentiary (full powers) of the United States of America, on the part and behalf of the said States, of the one part; and the undersigned King, Chiefs, and Warriors, of the Great and Little Osage Tribes or Nations, on the part and behalf of their said Tribes or Nations, of the other part.
>
> The parties being desirous of re-establishing peace and friendship between the United States and the said tribes or nations, and of being placed in all things, and in every respect, on the same footing upon which they stood before the war.

Among the many names of the Osage leaders who signed the treaty was "Wahadanoe"(*Wahadaniñe*) of the Missouris who were with the Little Osages. This was the first time a Missouria Indian had signed a treaty with the United States. In June of 1825 the Osages signed another treaty in St. Louis ceding their remaining lands in Missouri and Arkansas. A headman identified as "Khigaiswachinpichais, Missouri Chief," signed for his people. Within a few years, these Missouria were completely absorbed into Osage society. The Missouria and Otoe on the Platte River did not sign any treaty with the United States until June 24, 1817. Although they had remained neutral in the War of 1812, they were still pressured to affirm their loyalty to the United States, and they eventually complied.

> A treaty of peace and friendship made and concluded between William Clark and Auguste Chouteau, commissioners on the part, and behalf of the United States of America, of the one part; and the undersigned chiefs and warriors, of the Ottoes tribe of Indians, on the part and behalf of their said tribe, of the other part.
>
> THE parties being desirous of re-establishing peace and friendship between the United States and their said tribe and of being placed, in all things, and in every respect, upon the same footing upon which they stood before the late war between the United States and Great Britain, have agreed to the following articles:
>
> ARTICLE 1. Every injury or act of hostility by one or either of the contracting parties against the other, shall be mutually forgiven and forgot.
>
> ARTICLE 2. There shall be perpetual peace and friendship between all the citizens of the United States of America and all the individuals composing the said Ottoes tribe, and all the friendly relations that existed between them before the war, shall be, and the same are hereby, renewed.
>
> ARTICLE 3. The undersigned chiefs and warriors, for themselves and their said tribe, do hereby acknowledge themselves to be under the protection of the United States of America, and of no other nation, power, or sovereign, whatsoever. In witness whereof, the said William Clark and Auguste Chouteau, commissioners as aforesaid, and the chiefs aforesaid, have hereunto subscribed their names and affixed their seals, this twenty-fourth day of June, in the year of our Lord one thousand eight hundred and seventeen, and of the independence of the United States the forty-first.

A dozen Otoe chiefs signed the document, as did the Missouria chiefs: "Tarposta," Son of the Priest; "Kahhehpah" *Kax'epa*, Crow Head; "Harahkraton," the Sparrow Hawk; "Tawequa" *Taiñe*, the Little Deer; and "Chanohato" *Chenohato*, Buffalo Hump. The treaty language seems harmless since the Indians were giving up no land.

Major Long's Council with the Otoe Indians, 1819, by Samuel Seymour.
Major Stephen H. Long and Agent Benjamin O'Fallon met with the Otoe,
Missouria, and Ioway at Council Bluffs, Nebraska, on October 4, 1819. It
was at this council that O'Fallon tried to extinguish the independent identity of the Missouria. (Courtesy of the State Historical Society of Missouri)

However, Article 3 opened the door for the government to intervene
in Otoe and Missouria tribal affairs. Other treaties would soon follow, and those would require the tribes to cede land.

Major Stephen H. Long and government agents met with "100
Otoe, 70 Missouria, and 50 or 60 Ioway men" at the Council Bluffs
on October 4, 1819. This site was near William Clark's second meeting or "official" council with the Missouria and Otoe. The officials
watched the warriors "strike the post" with their tomahawks and
clubs and recount their war deeds before delivering their orations.
Agent Benjamin O' Fallon, a nephew of William Clark who became
known for his harsh treatment of Indians, refused to recognize the
Missouria headmen present, attempting to force the complete merg-
ing of the Missouria with the Otoe tribe. An aged Missouria headman named "Loutre" (Otter) Dosdange gave a long speech at the
conclusion of the proceedings in which he predicted his death. He
passed away within a few hours.

The January 7, 1820, edition of the *Missouri Intelligencer* printed
part of the speech of "the Great Missouri Chief" given at the council. This is possibly Otter's speech, but government agents and the
newspaper's editors have obviously made some changes. The chief
recalled a time "when our fathers and many of us lived in the full

enjoyment of the inestimable privileges handed down to us by our ancestors—the loss of which we now lament with bitter but unavailing regret." The chief said that when they compared their condition to former times, they felt nothing "but the deepest sense of mortification and sorrow." He lamented the encroachment of white settlers on their old domain and blamed this "evil spirit" on the massive New Madrid earthquake of 1811. The U.S. government had given people certificates to exchange the devastated farmland along the Mississippi River for new land in the "Boonslick Country" of central Missouri. Many of these New Madrid certificates were divided up and offered for sale. From 1816 onward, white settlers poured into the ancient Missouria homeland. Baptist Missionary John Mason Peck compared this immigration to "an avalanche."

The treaty of September 26, 1825, increased American intervention in Otoe and Missouria tribal affairs. Article 1 required the tribes to acknowledge that the United States had the right to regulate all their trade and commerce. Trade between the United States and New Mexico was booming, thanks to the Santa Fe Trail. Indian raiders posed a potential threat to the wagon caravans, especially those returning from Mexico with mules and horses. Superintendent of Indian Affairs Thomas McKinney reported the Otoe and Missouria had harassed some of the caravans. Article 2 directed the Otoe and Missouria,

> To give safe conduct to all persons who may be legally authorized by the United States to pass through their country. . . . Nor will they, whilst on their distant excursions, molest or interrupt any American citizen or citizens who may be passing from the United States to New Mexico, or returning from thence to the United States.

For its part, the government promised the Otoe and Missouria "the friendship and protection of the United States" and "benefits and acts of kindness as may be convenient, and seem just and proper to the President of the United States."

Dispossessed eastern tribes like the Potawatomie and the Sac and Fox were settled in western Iowa. The government had forced the Otoe and Missouria to cede this land in the 1830 Treaty of Prairie du Chien. The dispossessed eastern Indians hunted on other lands "reserved" by the government for Otoe and Missouria hunting grounds. The bison herds were shrinking in the Missouri valley, and the Otoe and Missouria had to range farther each year to find them. This put them in competition with the larger and more aggressive nations like the Lakota Sioux, Cheyenne, and Arapahoe. During their seasonal bison hunts the Missouria, Otoe, Omaha, and Pawnee often banded together for mutual protection.

Another treaty with the Otoe and Missouria was made on September 21, 1833. This treaty overtly attempted to turn the Indians from hunters into farmers:

> ARTICLE 6. The United States agree to deliver to said Otoes and Missouris, one thousand dollars value in stock, which shall be placed in the care of the agent, or farmer, until the President thinks the same can safely be entrusted to the Indians.
>
> ARTICLE 7 . . . the Otoes and Missouris shall locate themselves in such convenient agricultural districts, as the President may think proper, nor shall the payments be continued, if the Otoes and Missourias shall abandon such location as the President shall think best for their agricultural interest.
>
> ARTICLE 8. The Otoes and Missouris declare their entire willingness to abandon the chase for the agricultural life and their desire for peace with all other tribes, and therefore agree not to make war against any tribe with whom they now are.

The Otoe and Missouria may not have understood the full intent of the treaty or they may have been concerned primarily with getting merchandise through their agreement to it. They had no interest in abandoning hunting for an agricultural life. Neither could the government decree peace. While Otoe and Missouria were seldom the aggressors, warfare was still a primary means for young males to achieve manhood, and enemies surrounded them, including their former Osage and Kansa allies. Superintendent of Indian Affairs McKinney noted the exceptional bravery of the Otoe and Missouria in the face of such overwhelming odds.

6

The End of the
Missouria Homeland

On October 15, 1836, at Bellevue Agency in Nebraska, the Missouria, Otoe, Omaha, Yankton, and Santee Dakota signed a treaty by which they agreed to "for ever cede relinquish and quit claim to the United States all our right title and interest of whatsoever nature in and to the lands lying between the State of Missouri and the Missouri river . . ." This treaty was known as the "Platte Purchase" in which the U.S. acquired what became six counties in the northwest corner of Missouri. The Otoe and Missouria had to abandon their autumn buffalo hunt to attend the treaty council. To compensate for the disruption and prove the "good will and friendship" of the United States, agents John Dougherty and Joshua Pilcher agreed to give the Indians additional merchandise: "To the Otoes twelve hundred and fifty dollars, to the Missouries one thousand dollars to the Omahaws twelve hundred and seventy dollars. To the Yankton and Santee bands of Sioux one thousand dollars."

An earlier government directive for the Otoe and Missouria to move their villages farther west had prevented them from harvesting their crops. Now with the fall buffalo hunt disrupted, they faced the very real prospect of starvation over the winter. Dougherty and Pilcher added an emergency food ration to Article 3 of the treaty:

In consequence of the removal of the Otoes and Missouries from their former situation on the river Platte to the place selected for them, and of their having to build new habitations last spring at the time which should have been occupied in attending to their crops, it appears that they have failed to such a degree as to make it *certain* that they will lack the means of subsisting next spring, when it will be necessary for them to commence cultivating the lands now preparing for their use. It is therefore agreed that the said Otoes, and Missouries (in addition to the presents herein before mentioned) shall be furnished at the expense of the United States with five hundred bushels of corn to be delivered at their village in the month of April next.

Along with the Otoes, Missouria headmen "Hah-che-ge-sug-a"; *Gretun Thewe*, Black Hawk; *Nahje hinge*, No Heart; "Wan-ge-ge-he-ru-ga-ror," the Arrow Fender; "Wah-ne-min-er"; and *Ahuxañe*, Big Wing, signed the treaty to get the desperately needed food. Congress ratified the treaty, and President Andrew Jackson signed it on February 15, 1837, officially extinguishing all Missouria title and claim within the state of Missouri. The Platte Purchase rapidly filled with white settlers, and the wild game was quickly depleted.

From this point on, the history of the Nyut^achi is centered primarily in Nebraska, Kansas, and finally, Oklahoma. However, it is important to know what eventually became of the namesakes of the twenty-fourth state and the longest river in the United States.

Government agents and missionaries now lived in the Otoe and Missouria villages, and they tried to coerce the Indians into living like the Euro-Americans. Moses Merrill, a Baptist missionary to the Otoe and Missouria from 1833 to 1840, was genuinely concerned with their welfare, but missionaries often tended to equate the Christian faith with dressing and acting like New England farmers, an unappealing prospect to the Indians. Even worse, the Indians fell prey to the numerous whiskey peddlers now operating out of Missouri.

The impact of liquor on the Otoe-Missouria is a painful topic. Some of these problems have been noted in previous chapters. Alcohol not only destroyed individuals, it devastated an entire cultural fabric. Following warfare or an epidemic, a recovery was possible, but there could be no recovery from liquor. Unscrupulous traders and corrupt officials, whether French, Spanish, English, or American, often made sure liquor was available. Indians had no natural resistance to liquor's addictive qualities. Maximilian observed the cumulative

"Muncha-Huncha," Big Bear, also known as Joseph Powell, photograph by William Henry Jackson, ca. 1874. "A full-blooded Missouria
who succeeded his grandfather, Cow-h-pa-ha, as leader of the Bear
Clan in 1870. As a youth, he lived much of his time among the whites.
At the time of this photograph he was considered the 'leading sprit
of the Otoe and Missouria in the industrial pursuits of civilized life.'
This placed him at odds with the traditionalist in the tribe. He was
described as possessing a splendid physique and was nearly six feet
tall." (Courtesy of the Special Collections Department, University of
Iowa Libraries)

impact on the Otoe and Missouria in 1833. "All these Indians were weaker, and of lower stature, than those of the upper Missouri. . . . The Otoes and Missouris intended to go today with their stock of whiskey to their villages on the other side of the river." After visiting the Missouri whiskey peddlers, the Otoe-Missouria wanted Maximilian's party to ferry them across the river, but he refused. Moses Merrill elaborated further on the problems caused by whiskey:

> The Indians are excessively fond of ardent spirits and notwithstanding the laws of our land to the contrary, they are plentifully supplied. Their drunkenness leads to dissension and sometimes murder. At these seasons it is unsafe to be with them without an interpreter. The Indians exchange not only their furs for liquor but their horses, guns and blankets.

Merrill despaired because he saw the Indians "led away by their own lusts and by wicked white men whose sole object is worldly gain." A Methodist missionary, Reverend William H. Goode, laid the problem squarely at the feet of Euro-American culture:

> Often I have been compelled to ask myself, "Who is the civilized and who is the savage?" Their principal vices are emphatically our vices. If they get drunk it is upon our whiskey . . . And yet we claim to be "civilized" and freely deal out to them the epithet "savage."

Cultural stress on the Otoe-Missouria increased tribal factionalism. The Missouria broke off from the Otoe in 1839 and formed a separate village near the mouth of the Platte. Hunger now forced the Indians to subsist on what they could forage and government rations. Otoe and Missouria hunters entered Buchanan County in northwest Missouri in the winter of early 1840. This was probably one of the last times the Missouria were in their old homeland in an organized group. They slaughtered some settlers' cattle to feed their starving families. This led to a tense confrontation with U. S. Dragoons (mounted troops) from Fort Leavenworth under the command of Major Nathan Boone, the son of famed frontiersman Daniel Boone. A report in the April 4, 1840, *Missouri Argus* commended Major Boone for peaceably removing the Indians. The paper called for strengthening the garrison at Fort Leavenworth and building a new fort in the northwest corner of the state to protect the settlers from Indians.

Frustrated at losing their dignity as self-sufficient warriors and hunters, Otoe and Missouria men sometimes shot at passing boats

"Choncape" also known as "Big Kansas," portrait by Charles Bird King, 1821. Big Kansas was an important leader of the Otoe and Missouria in the first half of the nineteenth century. His headdress is a roach made of deer tail or horse hair and feather of a golden eagle, both dyed red. The mandibles and scalps of ivorybill and pileated woodpeckers adorn the headband. The war club is a form of the mace. These items demonstrate a link to the symbolism passed down from the Mississippian and Oneota cultures. (Courtesy of the State Historical Society of Missouri)

on the Missouri River. When confronted by government agents, Otoe-Missouria headman "Choncape" *Shunga pi,* Good Horse, also known as Big Kansas, defended his warriors, saying the harassment was a small price to pay for so many broken government promises. A shooting incident in September of 1844 resulted in two Otoe-Missourias being arrested and imprisoned at Fort Leavenworth. A sentinel later shot and killed one of the prisoners, who was allegedly trying to escape.

Major Clifton Wharton held a council with the Otoe-Missouria near Bellevue Agency, Nebraska, and issued a stern warning against shooting at boats. "If you continue to behave in this manner all the people will entertain an animosity towards you." He told the Indians they would be like "a lone tree upon the prairie" that had withstood many storms, but the last storm to come would "destroy them completely." Lieutenant Henry Carlton said the long-winded speech was "so much a dead loss to the Indians." The interpreter could not translate the full effect of the major's lengthy speech. Frustrated, the major finally said, "Tell them everybody will hate them, if they don't quit acting this way."

The government's simple solution to the ongoing crisis facing the Otoe-Missouria was twofold: First, get the Indians to quit hunting and grow more corn; second, increase their annuities (cash payments) and supplies by getting them to cede more of their land. Under the Treaty of 1854 the government assigned the Otoe and Missouria to a small reservation straddling the Big Blue River on the Kansas and Nebraska border, where they continued to follow their traditional lifestyle. Few had intermarried with whites; very few could speak any English; and much to the irritation of government officials, they refused to quit hunting buffalo.

Whereas the Christian missionaries primarily laid blame for the Otoe-Missouria alcohol problem on traders, Indian Commissioner George Manypenny placed responsibility on the Indians themselves. Manypenny sought to penalize the Indians under Article 10 of the 1854 Treaty, stating anyone "who drinks liquor, may have his or her proportion of the annuities withheld from him or her." What was to happen to those withheld funds was not made clear.

Conditions deteriorated throughout the 1850s, and conflicts with nomadic plains tribes increased. The stream of Euro-Americans into Indian country never lessened. An Osage headman characterized the white migration by saying, "They just keep coming like ants."

"Op-Ho-Hom-Mon-Ne," Buck Elk Walking, and "E'en-Brick-To," Black Bird, an Otoe-Omaha, photograph by William Jackson, ca. 1874. Buck Elk Walking (seated) is a full blood Missouria. Unlike the Colt revolver he is holding, his scalp lock, body tattoos, and dress reflect an older traditional style. His personal adornments such as beads, arm bands, and gorget are similar to those recovered at the Utz and Gumbo Point sites. Black Bird's clothing shows more adaptation of Euro-American fashion. His mixed heritage demonstrates how intertribal marriages became more common as Indian populations declined. (Courtesy of the National Anthropological Archives)

After the Civil War, settlers and railroad companies wanted the Otoe-Missouria removed. The Big Blue River reservation was considered some of the richest farmland and best timberland in the region, and a handsome profit could be made from it if the Indians were gone.

Agent Albert Langhorn Green observed in the late 1860s that the Otoe-Missouria were becoming more like the nomadic plains tribes in appearance and behavior. For example, most of the men grew their hair long instead of shaving the head in the traditional scalp lock. Less time was spent planting crops and more time hunting, searching for the shrinking bison herds. Often the Indians still had to subsist on foraging or government rations. Part of the tribe joined the Kansa summer buffalo hunt in 1874 without the permission of Agent Jesse Griest. *Shunge Xowe,* Medicine Horse, Little Pipe, and four other leaders were arrested by the U.S. Army and jailed at Fort Hays, Kansas. When they were finally released, the government deducted $1,000 from their annuities to pay the army's expenses.

The Otoe-Missouria went on their last buffalo hunt in the autumn of 1874 or some accounts say, 1876. They followed the Platte River almost into Wyoming. Twelve-year-old *Soje Yinge,* Little Smoke (Charles Washington Dailey), of the Missouria Eagle Clan, was taken along. He later gave his nephew Truman Dailey a detailed account of the ceremonial preparations and activities surrounding the hunt. Ironically, this hunt was a success, but white hide hunters soon eradicated the few remaining bison herds.

The Otoe-Missouria split over a disagreement about selling the Big Blue reservation. One group wanted to sell, move to Indian Territory (Oklahoma), and continue to live as Indians. Government officials called this group of traditionalists the "Coyote Band." The other group wanted to remain in Nebraska; its members tried to adapt to Euro-American farming methods. Many of their children attended mission schools. These became known as the "Quaker Band."

A government-sponsored sale of land on the Blue River Reservation in 1877 was a disaster, according to agent Jesse Griest. The Indians received none of the land payments, and white squatters overran tracts clearly occupied by Indian families. In 1878, members of the Coyote Band under Arkeketa, "Stand By It," went to the Indian Territory to find a home free from the pressure of white civilization. In 1880 about half of the Otoe-Missouria took up residence on the Cimarron River near the Sac and Fox reservation. Pressure grew to remove the Quaker Band to the Indian Territory.

On October 5, 1881, over 230 Otoe and Missouria, men, women, and children left Nebraska for a new reservation along Red Rock Creek in Indian Territory. They walked eighteen days before reaching their new home, driving their livestock ahead of them. Their relatives under Arkeketa eventually joined them there. The government then sold off the remaining tracts of the Blue River reservation. Only a few mixed heritage families remained in Nebraska on their allotted farms. The remainder of the reservation was sold, but the Indians did not receive payment from the sale until 1899. Many of the settlers' payments to the government were deferred, and only $120,000 of the $270,000 owed was paid to the Otoe-Missouria tribe.

Indian Territory did not prove to be a refuge from white civilization. As part of the pressure to force the Otoe-Missouria to assimilate, agents prohibited the tribe from practicing traditional ceremonies. By 1895, most Otoe-Missouria had adopted Euro-American methods of farming, and most adults could speak some English. Children were sent to government boarding schools and not allowed visits by their parents. They were physically punished if they spoke their native language or acted "Indian." When anthropology student William Whitman arrived in Red Rock in the spring of 1935 to record traditional Otoe-Missouria culture, George Washington Dailey and other tribal elders told him that he was fifty years too late.

What Whitman learned from his informants was based mostly on their memories of what their parents and grandparents had told them, rather than on their personal experience. He talked with only one elder who had been a member of the Buffalo Medicine Society. Others whom he was sure knew more would not talk with him. A century of abuse had caused them to distrust Americans, and what little sacred knowledge was left they were not to going to share with an outsider.

Most tribal members were reluctant to adopt all the values of Euro-American society. They clung to remaining fragments of the old culture. Close interaction among Indian tribes in Oklahoma led to a movement called "Pan-Indianism." Clothing, dances, and ceremonies of diverse tribes were combined to replace some of the tribal-specific traditional components that had been lost. Shrinking populations limited the marriage pool, so mates had to be sought from neighboring tribes. Young men and women from different tribes attending the same government schools also resulted in many intertribal marriages. The Native American Church, a blend of traditional Indian beliefs

"Thrach-Tche," True Eagle, photograph by William Henry Jackson, ca. 1875. "A full-blood Missouria, and nephew of Ah-ho-che-ka-thocka (Quapaw Indian Striker), a title gained by his bravery in battle against the Quapaws, and who was head chief. At his (Ah-he-cho-ka-thocka's) death, the hereditary successor, Good Talker, was assassinated by Shungech-hoy and others, when the line of descent fell on True Eagle, who became chief in 1860, and held the position of Missouria chief in the confederated Otoes and Missourias until 1874, when he resigned in favor of his nephew. Is now about 80 years of age, six feet in height, with a stout, well proportioned frame." (Courtesy of the Special Collections Department, University of Iowa Libraries)

and Christianity became an important institution for many Otoe-Missouria to maintain their "Indianess" in their worship after 1900. Even Otoe-Missouria tribal members who were Quakers, Catholics, or Protestants still maintained a certain degree of "Indian values."

Epilogue

Allotment and a New Beginning

During the 1890s, the federal government initiated a process called allotment. The Indian reservations were to be divided among tribal members in small acreages and the "surplus" land then sold to white settlers. The government was to hold the allotted lands and profits from the sale "in trust" for twenty-five years for the Otoe-Missouria. The Otoe-Missouria resisted allotment, but government officials threatened and harassed them to force compliance. The Otoe-Missouria in turn harassed the surveyors partitioning the reservation land and destroyed their survey markers.

In the summer of 1894, half of the Otoe-Missouria tribe reluctantly agreed to the allotment, fearful that otherwise the government would assign them poorer lands as punishment. In October, the government did exactly that to those who had resisted. Eighty-two thousand acres of reservation land was prepared for auction. Otoe-Missouria leaders went to Washington, D.C., and appealed to stop the allotment. On April 25, 1895, *Ketaⁿinge*, Little Turtle, known as Mitchell Deroin, of mostly Missouria and French descent, made an impassioned plea to Commissioner of Indian Affairs Thomas P. Smith:

> We are here in regard to our land. We ask you to ask the Secretary [of the Interior] not to sign any papers . . . that land we are living on was bought for the Otoe tribe with their own money . . . we cannot look back and live in lodges as we used to live. We must hold the plow and turn the ground . . . We do not kick about that; we have got to work for our living. That is all right. But let us hold

our land as it is now, I beg you. But if the government gives us our land in severalty, it will be out of our hands. . . . We can live like white men without cutting up our land. Look at us: you see me with pants and coat on, but we are Indians all the same. Why cannot we work like a white man and hold our land as it is? Future generations will say: "We had a home once and I wish my people had held that land." That is why I want this home for the generation to come. Let us send our children to school and let them learn to read and write. They are learning now and if they grow to be men they will want to hold that land worse than we do now.

Despite the pleas of Otoe-Missouria leaders, Smith simply replied that allotment would benefit the tribe and that the reservation would be broken up. An investigation in 1916 found that some government officials conspired with local businessmen to swindle the Indians out of their allotments. From 1917 to 1921, the federal government tried to get the Indians to apply for termination of the twenty-five-year "trust period." This meant the Otoe-Missouria tribe would "officially" cease to exist and the government would be relieved of all treaty obligations and cash payments due to the Indians.

When the government relented in 1922, most Otoe-Missouria were paying state and county taxes on their land, something that was never supposed to have happened under the allotment process. As the Otoe-Missouria feared, over 90 percent of their reservation land passed from their ownership. The federal government had proven once again that it either could not or would not adhere to the treaties and promises it made.

Some government officials genuinely believed that what they were doing was for the long-term good of the Otoe-Missouria. Others simply wanted them out of the way or saw their removal as a means to personal political or monetary gain. Government policies to "de-Indianize" and assimilate the Otoe-Missouria had a far more devastating impact on their culture than had the epidemics and wars with other Indian tribes. In those cases, they had always recovered to some degree and reconstituted their culture; however, government policies threatened the permanent loss of the language, sacred traditions, and knowledge of tribal history. Even as late as 1990, Truman Dailey expressed concern over what he saw as continued government interference "in our way of life and our religion."

Despite harsh treatment by the government and by some white neighbors, over two dozen Otoe-Missouria men served with the U.S.

This photograph of George Washington Dailey, Old Eagle of the Missouria Eagle Clan, was taken around 1930 at a Memorial Day service at the Otoe-Missouria cemetery at Red Rock, Oklahoma. Mr. Dailey demonstrates the close affinity the Missouria had for horses for many generations. (Courtesy of the Research Division of the Oklahoma Historical Society)

armed forces in World War I, although they were not even considered citizens of the United States until 1924. The old system of government by clan leadership gradually faded away and was replaced with an elected tribal council. The Otoe-Missouria people suffered greatly, as did most Oklahomans, in the "dust bowl" during the Great Depression of the 1930s. Legal actions presented by the Otoe-Missouria to the federal Indian Claims Commission in the 1950s resulted in payment of partial compensation for some treaties and land sales in which the tribe had been cheated.

Significant numbers of Otoe-Missouria men and women served in the European and Pacific theaters during World War II and later in Korea and Vietnam. For such a small tribe, the number of veterans' tombstones in the Otoe-Missouria cemetery at Red Rock makes a sobering and lasting impression. The Otoe-Missouria War Mothers Society, formed during World War II, honors and supports the modern day Otoe-Missouria warriors in a traditional manner through ceremonies, prayers, and physical support of the troops and their families.

Many Otoe-Missouria are reawaking to their cultural heritage in Missouri. Truman Dailey was the keynote speaker at the dedication of the Van Meter State Park visitors' center, now known as Missouri's American Indian Cultural Center on April 21, 1990. Dailey said, "I am the first of my people to ever come back. And it makes me feel good, as I walk where my people lived, to think I might set foot in one of their tracks." Since that time, several groups of Otoe-Missouria have visited the park and the Utz site, participating in educational programs at the center or conducting spiritual activities such as songs and prayers.

The descendants of the Nyut^achi, especially as part of the Otoe-Missouria Tribe of Oklahoma, continue to make their way and contribute to contemporary American society. The Otoe-Missouria tribe has about 2,200 enrolled members and invests in several business enterprises. Members face the same challenges and opportunities that most Americans do as well as some that are unique because they are a sovereign Indian nation. Despite three hundred years of cultural upheaval and devastation, the Otoe-Missouria people continue to honor traditions that reflect roots going back to their days on the Missouri River.

Truman Dailey playing the drum with the White Calf Singers at the dedication of the Van Meter visitors' center in 1990. Truman was the first person of Missouria descent to visit his ancestral home. (Courtesy of Jim Price, *Columbia Daily Tribune*)

Missouri's American Indian Cultural Center at Van Meter State Park. The Van Meter visitors' center was given a new mission and renamed in 2004. In addition to interpreting the history of the Missouria nation, the center seeks to improve public understanding of all the historic Indian nations that once resided in Missouri. (Courtesy of the Missouri Department of Natural Resources)

The Otoe-Missouria Tribal Seal bears the images of the seven surviving clans: the bear, eagle, beaver, bison, deer, owl, and pigeon. The clan totems surround a prayer feather. (Courtesy of the Otoe-Missouria Tribe of Oklahoma)

For Further Reading
and Research

There is no single book dealing exclusively with Missouria history and culture. Multiple resources must be gleaned for bits and pieces of information. Most historical publications carried stories about the Missouria that came from rather dubious sources. These erroneous stories, sometimes reprinted as factual descriptions of events, have become an interesting part of Missouri folklore.

Books

- *1491: New Revelations of the Americas before Columbus,* by Charles C. Mann (New York: Knopf-Doubleday, 2005).

- *Before Lewis and Clark, Documents Illustrating the History of the Missouri, 1785–1804,* by Abraham P. Nasatir (Lincoln: University of Nebraska Press, 1990).

- *Cahokia: Ancient America's Great City on the Mississippi,* by Timothy R. Pauketat (New York: Viking Penguin, 2009).

- *Hero, Hawk, and Open Hand: American Indian Art of the Ancient Midwest and South,* by Richard Townsend, general editor (New Haven and London: Art Institute of Chicago and Yale University Press, 2004).

- *A History of the Osage People* by Louis F. Burns (Tuscaloosa: University of Alabama Press, 2004).

- *The Imperial Osages: Spanish-Indian Diplomacy in the Mississippi Valley,* by Gilbert Din (Norman: University of Oklahoma Press, 1983).

- *Indians and Archaeology of Missouri,* by Carl H. Chapman and Eleanor F. Chapman (Columbia: University of Missouri Press, 1983).

- *The Ioway Indians,* by Martha Royce Blaine (Norman: University of Oklahoma Press, 1979).

- *Jiwele-Baxoje Wan'Shige Ukeny Ich': Otoe-Iowa Indian Language,* volumes I and II, *Otoe and Iowa Language Speakers,* by Lila Wistrand-Robinson & Jimm GoodTracks (Park Hill OK: Jilwele—Baxoje Language Project, 1978).

- *Letters of the Lewis and Clark Expedition with Related Documents,* by Donald Jackson (Champaign: University of Illinois Press, 1978).

- *One Vast Winter Count,* by Colin G. Calloway (Lincoln: University of Nebraska Press, 2003).

- *The Osage: The Children of the Middle Waters,* by John Joseph Mathews (Norman: University of Oklahoma Press, 1961).

- *Osage Indian Customs and Myths,* by Louis F. Burns (Fallbrook, CA: Ciga Press, 1984).

- *The Oto,* by William Whitman (New York: Columbia University Press, 1937).

- *The Otoes and Missourias: A Study of Indian Removal and the Legal Aftermath,* by Basil Berlin Chapman (Oklahoma City: Times Journal Publishing, 1965).

- *The Otoe-Missouria Elders: Centennial Memoirs (1881–1981)* (Red Rock, OK: Otoe-Missouria Tribe, 1981).

- *The Otoe-Missouria People,* by David Edmunds (Phoenix, AZ: Indian Tribal Series, 1976).

- *The Petroglyphs and Pictographs of Missouri,* by Carol Diaz Granados and James Duncan (Tuscaloosa: University of Alabama Press, 2000).

- *Seeking a Newer World: The Fort Osage Journals and Letters of George Sibley 1808–1811,* edited by Jeffrey E. Smith (St. Charles, MO: Lindenwood University Press, 2003).

- *The Spanish Regime in Missouri,* by Louis B. Houck (Chicago: R.R. Donnelly & Sons, 1909).

- *Wahtohtana heda Nyut^achi Mahin Xanje akipa (The Year the Otoe and Missouria Meet the Americans), by* Matthew Jones (Lincoln, NE: self-published, 2004).

Archives

- *Glenn A. Black Laboratory of Archaeology* University of Indiana, Bloomington, IN

- *Illinois Historical Society,* Springfield, IL (Quotations from *Transactions of the Illinois State Historical Society)*

- *Joint Collections, State Historical Society of Missouri—Western Historical Manuscripts Collection,* Columbia, MO

- *Missouri History Museum, Library and Research Center,* St. Louis MO (Original and microfilmed copies of records for Spanish Illinois-Louisiana)

- *Nebraska State Historical Society,* Lincoln, NE

- *Oklahoma Historical Society,* Oklahoma City, OK

  Smithsonian Institution, National Anthropological Archives Washington, D.C.

- *State Historical Society of Missouri,* Columbia, MO (Many quotations used in the text came from issues of the *Missouri Historical Review* and newspapers in the society's collections).

Articles

- "Development and Interrelationships of Oneota Culture in the Lower Missouri Valley" by Dale R. Henning, The Missouri Archaeologist, vol. 32 (December 1970)

- "Ducharme's Invasion of Missouri an Incident in the Anglo-Spanish Rivalry for the Indian Trade of Upper Louisiana," by Abraham P. Nasatir, *Missouri Historical Review,* vol. 24, nos. 1, 2, 3.

- "The Kaskaskia Manuscripts: French Traders in the Missouri Valley before Lewis and Clark," by Theresa J. Piazza, *Missouri Archaeologist,* vol. 53 (December 1992).

- *The Little Osage and Missouri Indian Village Sites ca. 1727–1777 A.D.*, by Carl H. Chapman, *Missouri Archaeologist*, vol. 21, no. 1 (December 1959).

- "The Missouri Indians," J. Brewton Berry, *Southwestern Science Quarterly*, vol. 17, no. 2 (September 1936).

- "The Missouri Indian Tribe in Archaeology and History," by Robert T. Bray, *Missouri Historical Review*, vol. 55, no 3 (April 1961).

- "An Oneota Site in Missouri," by J. Brewton Berry and Carl H. Chapman, *American Antiquity*, vol. 7, no. 3 (1942).

- "Tobacco Pipes of the Missouri Indians," by Henry W. Hamilton, Memoir No. 5, *Missouri Archaeological Society* (1967).

- "The Utz Site: An Oneota Village in Central Missouri," by Robert Bray, *Missouri Archaeologist*, vol. 52 (December 1991).

Unpublished Manuscripts

- "Black Otter's Narrative: Wisconsin Native Recollections Relating to Pre-History of the Lewis-Clark Expedition," by Frank Weinhold (Madison, WI, 2007)

- "Indian Path of Life: A Life History of Truman Washington Dailey of the Otoe-Missouria Tribe," by Lori Stanley (Columbia: University of Missouri, Ph.D. dissertation, 1993).

- "La decouverte du Missouri et l'histoire du Fort d'Orleans (1673–1728) (The Discovery of the Missouri and the History of Fort Orleans, 1673–1728)," by Baron Marc Villiers du Terrage, 1925, translated by Harriet Hopkins, from the archives of Robert Bray, transcribed by W. Raymond Wood.

- "Magnetic Survey of a Potential Location for the Ancient Missouri Village Site Noted by the Corps of Discovery in 1804 in Chariton County, Missouri," by Steven L. Devore (Midwest Archeological Center, National Park Service, Lincoln, NE, 2009).

- "Negotiating Identity: The Missouria's Response to European Contact 1670–1800," by Adam Fracchia (Columbia: University of Missouri, Masters Thesis, 2006).

- "Osage and Missouri Indian Life: Cultural Change 1675–1825," by Carl H. Chapman, project director, Leonard Blake et al. (Columbia: University of Missouri, 1985).

Online Resources

- *The Encyclopedia of Hotcak (Winnebago) Mythology,* Richard Dieterle, http://hotcakencyclopedia.com/
- *Indian Affairs: Laws and Treaties* Charles Kapplan, editor, http://digital.library.okstate.edu/kappler
- *Ioway Cultural Institute,* Lance Foster, http://ioway.nativeweb.org/home.htm
- *Ioway Otoe-Missouria Language,* Jimm Goodtracks, http://iowayotoelang.nativeweb.org/index.htm
- *The Jesuit Relations and Allied Documents 1610–1791,* Reuben Gold Thwaites, editor, http://puffin.creighton.edu/jesuit/relations/
- *The Journals of the Lewis and Clark Expedition,* Gary E. Moulton, editor, http://lewisandclarkjournals.unl.edu/
- *Missouri Archaeological Society* http://associations.missouristate.edu/mas/
- *Otoe-Missouria Tribe* http://www.omtribe.org/
- Wisconsin Historical Society Digital Collections http://content.wisconsinhistory.org/index.php

Museums Featuring Missouria Artifacts

- *Arrow Rock State Historic Site,* PO Box 1, Arrow Rock, MO 65320 http://www.mostateparks.com/arrowrock.htm
- *Missouri's American Indian Cultural Center,* Van Meter State Park, PO Box 128, Miami, MO 65344 http://www.mostateparks.com/vanmeter.htm

Index

About the Author

Michael Dickey is the Historic Site Administrator for the Division of State Parks of the Missouri Department of Natural Resources. He is the author of *Arrow Rock: Crossroads of the Missouri Frontier* and lives in Arrow Rock, Missouri.